THE
WALKER
WAY

A family's journey of loving people,
loss, and lawn mowers

BOB WALKER

FLUENCY
TELLING STORIES THAT MATTER

Produced with the assistance of Fluency Organization, Inc. Interior by Inkwell Creative

Everyone loves a story, and *The Walker Way* is a wonderfully engaging story of life, business, genuine faith, and lessons learned. From farm life to an international business, with plenty of twists and turns along the way, the journey of the Walker family is truly inspiring. Their guiding principles—to stay on course, stay true to one's values, and hold steady during the hard times, is a formula for all who seek to build a business, raise a family, and live a life of blessing.

Dr. John C. Bowling
Former President, Olivet Nazarene University
Bourbonnais, Illinois

A gritty story of courageous leadership, tenacious innovation and values, and a transformational vision. *The Walker Way* embodies a family's relentless generational commitment to delivering a high quality, reliable product at a great price. As you read these pages, you'll be equipped, inspired, and encouraged to be a leader that perseveres despite the challenges.

Dr. Dennis Rainey
Founder of FamilyLife
Little Rock, Arkansas

The Walker Way is a wonderful story of faith, family, inventiveness, perseverance, and the power of hard work and human spirit. It is filled with countless lessons and ideas that will make any business, large or small, better. As a supplier partner to the Walker family for over 60 years, we can say that there is no company we work with around the world in any of our industries that sets the quality and integrity bar higher. It's an honor and privilege to be a small part of *The Walker Way*.

David Kohler
President and Chief Executive Officer, Kohler Company
Kohler, Wisconsin

The Walker story is an insightful and moving account of the trials and tribulations of starting a business from the 50s through today. I can picture Bob Walker delivering parts in a Cadillac! Illustrating using whatever resources that are available, I saw many parallels with my family's experience in developing a company.

E. Stanley Guyer
President, The Grasshopper Company
Moundridge, Kansas

You will want to read this story of a great American company that arose from losing a business to great success, producing the premium zero turn mower in the industry. As a customer, I have seen the Walker Way exhibited as they care for people and make them a part of the Walker family. I left a 21-year career at Bank of America to operate my own landscape business. The Walker's unsurpassed products have given me and thousands of other Walker owners the opportunity to live our own (American) dream of doing something we love and supporting our families/making money at it. Discover the principles you can use in your own life and business, which this family-owned company has used to grow and prosper. You will enjoy this story of perseverance, innovation, and faith.

Bob Vickery
Owner, The Planters Touch
Easley, South Carolina

After reading *The Walker Way* a person should understand why we have viewed Walker Manufacturing as our #1 customer for more than 25 years, even when our sales to other companies may have been greater. They practice their beliefs daily in all aspects of their business. Other companies claim they want a working partnership with their suppliers, but Walker Manufacturing actually does it. This book tells you why we consider Walker Manufacturing to be the model for what we at Farrar Corporation look for in a customer.

Joe E. Farrar
President, Farrar Corporation
Norwich, Kansas

The Walker Way is one of those books that grips your heart and urges the reader to take action. Bob's words not only make you want to own a Walker Mower, but also to reevaluate your purpose in life and seek out what God may have for your future. The stories entertain, convict, and provide the perfect backdrop for the timeless principles that define the Walker legacy. Be forewarned: It will be hard to walk away from this book unchanged.

Anne-Renee Gumley
Co-author, *Shiny Things: Mothering on Purpose in a World of Distractions*
Proud supporter of her husband, Andrew Gumley, in his business: Walker Mowers of Alaska

What a joy to read this book about the Walker Way. The history of the Walker and Bandimere families are very similar. My prayer is that the Lord will use this book to help the next generations, to know that Hard Work does pay off, and that sticking with family through thick and thin makes a huge difference in the end of our stories! To God be the glory, great things he has done.

John Bandimere, Jr.
Bandimere Speedway
Morrison, Colorado

Faith, family, perseverance, the dignity of work. *The Walker Way...* The American way. This is a must-read for anyone who owns a business. If you are young and have dreams and aspirations, read this book. I have known Bob Walker for 10 years, and he has had such a positive influence on my life, as well as my son and daughter-in-law. I will have my grandchildren read his story.

Bill Chionio
President, Business Owners International
Estes Park, Colorado

This book is an epic story of the blessings a Christ-centered free market country can provide to anyone willing to step up and make it happen. The strength of Walker to remain steadfast in principles of faith and the execution of the American dream is truly inspirational. A must-read in our current national environment where capitalism is under attack.

Mike Lynch
Colorado State Representative
President, Western Heritage Company
Loveland, Colorado

A commitment to irresistible superiority and uncompromising quality is foundational to Walker Manufacturing products. Likewise, I found the wisdom of this book irresistible and uncompromising in its foundation on God's Word. Like a breath of fresh mountain air, this book will give the leader a clear head and inspiration to see their business anew as a holy calling with eternal impact.

Dale Lunsford, Ph.D.
Chancellor, LeTourneau University
Longview, Texas

After touring Walker Manufacturing several years ago, Bob told me with a smile, "We don't make lawn mowers; we make beautiful places." But it's not just the beauty of a well-manicured, Walker-mowed lawn. In *The Walker Way*, you'll see that one of those beautiful places is the company where the Walker family builds exceptional lawn equipment. Any business owner or would-be entrepreneur who wants to produce lasting value will do well to take heed to Bob's story of how loving people, hard work, and most of all, faith, fueled his family and Walker Manufacturing through seven decades and three generations.

Dr. Bill Peel
President and Founder, Foundations for Living/24Seven Project
Dallas, Texas

I am not a member of the family, but reading *The Walker Way* made me feel like a friend of the family. I believe more is caught than taught. In reading this book I caught a lot: insights on innovation, determination, problem-solving, service, succession planning, employee retention, utilizing technology, and the importance of character rooted in faith in God, his Word, and keeping one's word. Rarely does one get to sit with leaders in a multi-generation business. *The Walker Way* is just that opportunity and more. I highly recommend it.

Dr. Tommy Kiedis
President, Lancaster Bible College | Capital Seminary & Graduate School
Lancaster, Pennsylvania

The Walker Way is inspiring. It is a composite of the history of Walker Manufacturing Company, ethics, and sound business models, and it has a delightful spiritual foundation. This is a must-read book for any businessman or any person who wants to explore the secrets of success.

Dale L. Cutler
President, Cutler's Inc.
Orem, Utah

This book is dedicated to my parents, Max and Margaret Walker. Without their pioneering spirit, faith in God, courage, risk-taking, and the dream to be independent, there would be no story to share, and thousands of lives would not have been impacted by Walker Manufacturing Company.

Table of Contents

Foreword   13
Acknowledgements   19
Introduction   23

Chapter 1: Roots   25
    Fork in the road #1   27
    Early start   28
    Fork in the road #2   30
    The Power Truck   34
    Kansas struggles   37
    Move to Casper   40
    Waiting   41
    Back in business with cab coolers   42
    Experimental projects   44

Chapter 2: Small Beginnings   49
    The first prototypes   51
    Marketing lesson   53
    Toward independence   55
    Best opportunity   57

Chapter 3: Building Blocks 61
    Building a market 64
    Walker Talk magazine 69
    Celebrating 72
    Dan Walker, loss 76
    Our family 77

Chapter 4: In Search of Perfection 79
    Deck discipline 82
    Trial and error 85

Chapter 5: Preparing Family Leaders 87
    Learning curve 103
    Different paths 104
    Dean, Ted, and Ryan 106
    Hand-off 110

Chapter 6: The Great Recession 115
    Lessons learned 116
    Dignity of reply 118
    Day of rest 120

Chapter 7: Independent Thinking 123
    Growing too fast 124
    Having good instincts 125
    Carrot and a stick 127
    Entrepreneurial vision 128

Chapter 8: Your Best Opportunity 131
    Our product 133
    Being a specialist 134

Becoming a servant-leader   136

Chapter 9: Building a Foundation   139
  Being a good customer   140
  Doing business family-style   142
  Fear and faith   145
  Answering the big question   146
  Humble beginnings   149

Chapter 10: Beliefs Guide Us   153
  Staying enthused   158
  Creating jobs   160
  Small, slow beginnings   162

Chapter 11: Working Together   165
  Having a good name   168
  Showing gratitude/being generous   170
  Being dependable   171
  Building strong relationships   172
  Continuing investment   173
  Manufacturing technology   175
  Switching roles and best opportunities   177
  Skateboards   178
  Beautiful places   179
  The journey   180

Epilogue   181
Endnotes   185
About the Author   187
Additional Resources   189

Foreword

In the summer of 1992, at the International Lawn and Garden Expo in Louisville, Kentucky, I had the pleasure of meeting Bob Walker and his father, Max. I was a sophomore at Colorado State University in Fort Collins, Colorado, and because we lived in the same town, Bob was keen for me to visit the factory for a tour when my schedule allowed. I toured the factory the following January, and Bob and I spent six (yes, six) hours together touring the plant and sitting in his office just talking. We talked about everything from how and where we were raised, our families, what we each believe, and even our shared interest in gospel hymns—a staple in each of our upbringings. Little did I know I would spend many hours sitting in that same chair over the next 27 years under the leadership of a great man who was part of an incredible family.

It has been a distinct joy of mine over this time

to not only get to know Bob as a leader, father figure, and brother in Christ, but I have also come to know the Walker family. Bob's parents, Max and Margaret, made a great impact on me as I learned their entrepreneurial history, but also watched as they loved people and were some of the most unassuming folks I have ever known. They were authentic. Truly, you would have never picked out Max and Margaret as founders and owners of a multi-million-dollar, worldwide manufacturing company. But their impact on the people they came in contact with would affect many lives, as the Lord had richly enlarged their territory. They both had a way of engaging people of all types no matter if it was a potential customer, a struggling employee, or a delivery person they were encouraging to stay for one of our company lunches. For them, these engagements were the fruit of one thing—they just loved people.

The same authenticity and love for people that Max and Margaret lived out have been demonstrated by their children. I have been blessed to work closely with Bob and Dean over the years, and I have witnessed their humble joy for the success of the business and also for the success of the people who have made Walker Manufacturing a part of their lives. Bob and Dean have carefully (and quietly) worked to avoid bringing attention to themselves for the success of Walker Manufacturing, but rather to God, whom they freely call the CEO of this company. I have also been behind closed doors during the tough times (2009), and the primary takeaway from this dreadful time was that they both love people just like their parents did before them. Because of terrible economic conditions at that time, tough decisions had to be made, but it was (and remains) always through the lens that people matter the most.

In the same way that I have seen loving people as a priority for the Walker family, I have also witnessed an unquenchable thirst for excellence that I have seen in very few places. I have never seen the Walker family settle for "good enough"—even in the little things. Rather, I have witnessed a curiosity matched with God-given ingenuity that often brings about incredible solutions that many of us would have never imagined. Each time a success is achieved, credit and thanks are given to the One who is recognized as the source of their help.

I am happy to say that these same traits are alive and well in the third generation of Walkers. I have known these young men since they were children and teenagers, and as they have matured and moved into leadership in the business, they have done it with the same gracious and humble attitudes as the Walker generations before them. They have brought their own style of leadership while maintaining the same values that have built this company. Simple things like singing the *Doxology* as a leadership team at the end of our monthly finance meetings have recalled their roots while setting the tone for a new generation. Their posture of gratitude for what has been given to them, and their covenant to hand an even better business to a fourth Walker generation is easy to see. Their tenacity for excellence and the improvement of the state of the art, while pursuing customers, makes it an exciting time to be a part of Walker Manufacturing.

To be sure, *The Walker Way* is not just a book on the history of Walker Manufacturing and a memoir of how God has richly blessed this faithful family. It is a book on servant leadership, integrity, sound business principles, and authentic values that have been lived out daily for over half a century, well before writing a page of this book. I trust that you will find *The Walker Way* to be a good record of the journey of this amazing family, along with an understanding of the leadership style they have chosen that includes the value of others, faithfulness, optimism, and an unrelenting hunger for excellence.

Enjoy!

Tim

Tim Cromley started as an intern at Walker Manufacturing in September 1994 and was hired full-time in December of that year. He is the Marketing Manager.

Acknowledgements

I like to write and tell stories, but writing a book and getting it in print has turned out to be much more than that. This book would not have happened without the help and support of many others, and I want to say thank you.

First, I want to thank all of the employees, past and present, of Walker Manufacturing who have helped us design, manufacture, and sell and service our products across the years. Also, thanks goes to our worldwide network of distributors and dealers who provide service and support to our customers. The Lord has blessed me with the love and support of my family. My dear wife of 54 years, Barbara Ann, has stood with me through it all, and we have three wonderful daughters, Amy, Janey, Carey, and their husbands, David Stratton, Andrew Malander, and Ryan Doore. Each daughter has two boys and one girl—giving us nine grandchildren who keep me optimistic and looking forward. In addition to my family, the experience that is the basis of this book has been shared with my parents; my brother Dean and his wife, Suzanne; my sisters, Ruth Walker Saunders and Nina Walker Rattle, and their husbands, Dave and John; and my nephews (Dean and Suzanne's sons) Ted, Ryan, and Kyle.

Next, I would recognize Tim Cromley, Marketing Manager at Walker Manufacturing, who has long encouraged me to write the Walker story. Tim came to work in the company right after graduating from Colorado State University. It was his idea to develop a little booklet called the "Story of Walker" to hand out with our marketing materials for those who would like to know the company's history. This became the precursor to this book.

My editor and friend, Rod Dickens, who co-wrote the book with me and helped make the manuscript easy to read, is much appreciated for his talents as a writer, editor, and storyteller. I have known Rod for many years, as we first met when he was the chief editor for several trade publications in the landscape maintenance and outdoor power equipment industries. Rod was employed by the publishing company that has produced the *Walker*

Talk magazine, and he became the primary editor for all 56 issues of *Walker Talk*. I am very grateful for Rod's collaboration in producing this book.

I am recognizing the work of six proofreaders in raising the quality of this publication: Ann Waller, Al Heydorn, Gregg Wartgow, Suzanne Walker (my sister-in-law), Ruth Walker Saunders (my sister), and Debbie Rothgery (Walker Manufacturing Planning Manager). Each one improved the readability, accuracy, and English rendering of the manuscript.

Finally, our book publisher, Mary Ann Lackland, and her company, Fluency, have given us invaluable guidance in the process of getting this book into print. When we first met, she told me she loves books, and this passion shows in her work.

To all of you, thank you. May the Lord be praised.
Robert W. Walker

Introduction

Across the years there has been the occasional comment, "You ought to write a book." So here I am, taking the challenge to write down our journey, stories, and lessons learned after telling them quite a few times. In fact, looking back, some of the stories are getting better with time, and some of the hard things we faced are not so heavy as they once were.

I believe that telling of a journey, telling stories, and telling lessons learned is all wound up in the giving of ourselves to be a helper to others on their journeys. As is often said, "You can't make this stuff up," and the best stories are the real stories that have been lived in their times and circumstances. For people of faith, we believe that God created each of us with a plan in mind for our life—it is up to us to discover the plan and live our life to the fullest extent of God's plan. Of course, mistakes are made, and human frailty often is a part of the story, and that needs to be told, as well, so that lessons can be learned and mistakes not repeated.

Another motivation for writing down our journey is to help the company move into the future with family leadership. Future family leaders can be helped on their journey by building on the business foundation laid by their forebears and taking note of the earlier times and lessons learned. The times will be different for each generation, but time-tested principles will still guide and show the way—the **Walker Way**.

CHAPTER 1

Roots

*Grandpa showed me how to face loss and
how to forgive, one of many important lessons
our family has learned over the years, all of
which have played an important role in the
evolution and growth of our company.*

W hen we first started making lawn
mowers in 1980, we started off slowly
by manufacturing and selling a handful
of machines in our home state of Colorado and
eventually establishing a small network of dealers
in the neighboring states of Kansas, Oklahoma, and
Nebraska.

Within eight years, though, we had established a distributor/dealer network that covered the USA and we had developed an international export market. Today we build a machine, and sell and service a machine, every 20 to 25 minutes thanks to our factory employees, a network of 47 distributors, and 1,200 dealers around the world.

The Walker Mower story began long before 1977 when we made our first prototype mower. In fact, its roots extend all the way back to Fowler, Kansas, where my dad, Max, was farming along with my grandpa, Wesley Walker, and two uncles. Fowler is located about 30 miles southwest of Dodge City, and the farm raised cattle and grew grain and hay.

I was a teenager when my grandpa Walker's farm shed that stored the hay caught fire from spontaneous combustion. When the city fire engine pulled up it was not to fight the fire but to protect the town in case the fire spread; the shed, unfortunately, was located right across the highway from the town line. The firefighters refused to cross the line and fight the fire. Instead, they watched the shed burn.

Firefighters from neighboring towns eventually arrived, but they were too late. Several community residents were disgusted and could not understand why the local firefighters acted as they did. But Grandpa never complained and kept the right spirit. He ran an advertisement in the local newspaper the next week thanking those who had tried to help. In his thank you he quoted Scripture—"the Lord gave, and the Lord has taken away; blessed be the Name of the Lord" (Job 1:21b, ESV).

Grandpa showed me how to face loss and how to forgive, two of many important lessons our family has learned over the years, all of which have played an important role in the evolution and growth of our company.

Fork in the road #1

When my dad was in high school, he learned to play the trumpet and developed a love of the music of the early '40s—the sweet music and swing sound of the Big Band Era. He and a few friends formed their own little band. I don't know if the band ever played at an event, but they enjoyed jam sessions. This passion and interest built up to the point where Dad thought being a musician and entertainer would be his career choice after high school.

This was a fork in the road for Dad, and he told us he became convinced that the Lord did not want him to pursue the musical career. For Dad, it became a choice of following either God's plan for his life or pursuing music, and there was a moment of surrender when Dad said yes to God. How different our families' lives would have been if my dad had sung the old Frank Sinatra song "My Way" as his motto. Later, I remember Dad telling me, "It's awfully hard to make a living in the music business unless you make it big." In my estimation, my dad probably could have made it "big," but that was not in the Lord's plan.

Early start

Most farmers have skills that go far beyond raising cattle, harvesting hay and grain, and predicting weather. My dad was one of them. After seeing a miniature Caterpillar kit advertised in *Popular Mechanics*, he built a bulldozer for me in our farm shop using simple tools. I was only seven years old when Dad presented the gift to me at Christmas, and I still have the little bulldozer as a reminder of how gifted he was early on at designing and building machines. My brother, Dean, and I had many hours of enjoyment digging holes and filling them in with the little bulldozer.

Growing up on a family farm with four families to feed—our family, two uncles, and my grandparents—times were lean. But Dad never dwelled on the subject. He was always looking to take what he had in his hands and get started. Still, just as today, there was a limit back then as to how many family members a family farm could support.

Farming was getting bigger and fewer families were needed to operate the farm. My mother, Margaret, and my dad were aware of these limitations. Coupled with their desire to be independent, they started looking for other opportunities. One that kept coming to mind was manufacturing. At the time, there were many small manufacturing businesses in Kansas; often they were producing products related to agriculture. All Dad needed was an idea, and a salesman friend gave him one, building a gasoline-powered golf car. He told Dad, "You build the golf car, and I will sell it for you."

Fork in the road #2

Before fully committing to starting a manufacturing company, my parents were pursuing another life-altering choice. The parents of my dad's best friend in school had immigrated from Old Mexico. His parents did not speak English, and while spending time with the family, my dad learned to speak Spanish. My dad had a life-long special place in his heart for the Mexican people, one that likely came, in part, from this experience. Note: When interviewing a person for a job at Walker Manufacturing, if the person spoke Spanish, my dad would speak a little Spanish with them, both to keep in practice and to welcome the job applicant.

After my parents married, they developed some contacts with Christian missions in the Rio Grande Valley of South Texas. Sensing they were being called to work in a Christian mission in Mexico, they applied to a mission organization in McAllen, Texas. In 1957, on a vacation trip to South Texas, my parents interviewed with the mission organization. The mission turned my folks down and the door was shut.

The mission interviewer told Mom and Dad they did not have the educational credentials needed. When discussing the unfulfilled call to missions, my parents said they believed the Lord was testing them to see if they would be willing to serve (which they were). With that turn of events, my folks came home and set about starting the manufacturing company.

Dad was never interested in golf, neither watching nor playing it, but the idea of manufacturing a golf car intrigued him. He found the current electric-powered golf cars had a rather boxy design, and their batteries often failed to stay charged long enough to complete a round or two of play in the rental fleet.

After going to the drawing board, he came up with a rather unique design that stood apart in the market: The Walker Executive, a golf car with sweeping French curves and that was powered by a quiet gasoline engine. Dad's unique design also included a tilt-up body for easy maintenance and a simple, rugged driveline with an automatic variable-speed transmission.

From 1957 to 1963, Walker built approximately 1,000 of these innovative golf cars (some are still in use today). For the last three years, they were produced in our first manufacturing facility, a 48-ft.

by 80-ft. industrial building constructed only 100 ft. south of our farmhouse. Dad always said that back then one did not need a building permit to put up a new structure. He simply scraped off a little spot for the building pad with the farm's bulldozer and started building. At the time, I was in the 6th grade, and my brother was five years younger.

Dad started manufacturing with what he had available to him, and that was humble beginnings. The first golf cars were built in the small farm shop and the tools were simple: a hacksaw, cutting torch, electric welder, electric grinder, and a mulberry tree growing close by. The fork in the mulberry tree was used to bend and shape the tubing for the golf car body and frame. In the first couple of years, Dad continued to work on the farm full-time while producing golf cars late into the night. If someone had looked at where the golf cars were being produced, they would have been amazed at the origins of such a nice, finished product; Dad had an eye for quality and perfection in his DNA.

Mom had her part in getting the manufacturing company started. Although she had no formal training in operating a business or in bookkeeping, that did not stop her from getting a textbook or two on bookkeeping and self-teaching. She took pride in balancing the books to the penny. All the business office functions were accomplished by her hand, and at the same time, she managed to raise four kids.

Dean and I have shared in our appreciation of the lessons Mom and Dad learned in starting the business and how that has benefitted us. One lesson illustrated some of the business basics my parents learned the hard way. As farmers, they would go to work when the sun came up and quit when the sun set. When they started the manufacturing business, employees were told they could work as many hours as they wanted. That was the way they operated until an auditor was going over the books and noticed that overtime was not being paid. My folks had not heard of the wage and hour laws and overtime pay. There were some back wages to be paid and a lesson was learned.

Getting involved in the golf car business gave Dad, me, and my brother the opportunity to visit country clubs in Kansas City, Wichita, and Tulsa. It was eye-opening for farm boys to see a way of life that was very different from living in a small town in western Kansas where we were very sheltered.

A side note here. Dad had contracted with a man

from Kansas City to be a sales agent for the golf car. On one occasion, my dad and I met him at the Kansas City Country Club where he was a member. While giving us a tour, he took us to the locker room where he, upon opening his locker, offered Dad a drink from his stash of whiskey. Dad said he didn't drink, at which point the man made fun of him.

I remember this vividly because the drinking eventually ruined this man's life and he died of alcoholism. It made me very sad and left a huge impression on me. We do not condemn or judge how anyone else lives, but our family has lived a sober life. We never wanted alcohol to harm any family member and our thought has always been, if you don't touch it, you won't have a problem. That sounds like an extreme position, and it is, but it has always made sense to us.

The Power Truck

Realizing the golf car market was limited by its size and seasonality, Dad began looking for a product with a bigger market and application. He found it when he started to design and build a utility truck as a golf-car spinoff. To help fund the new Walker Power Truck, he sold the golf car's design rights and tooling to a group in Salina, Kansas. The company was Jato, Inc., and they produced the Walker Executive for several more years before going off the market. It is amazing that after 60 years, we still have people contact us about the golf car and tell us they have a Walker Executive.

As for the Power Truck, it could be used not only in agriculture, but also in industrial plants, airports, and resorts, in addition to being used on golf courses. It certainly had more market potential, and it also appealed to Dad's appetite for designing a wide range of configurations and attachments. Among them was a Power Truck with a pizza oven on the back for a franchise pizza delivery business, an idea that never came to fruition for an Indiana entrepreneur.

Dad also designed and built trams with sunroofs that could be towed by the Power Truck to ferry around amusement park visitors. He even developed a prototype for a mail delivery truck.

When the Power Truck was being developed, there were several other utility trucks already on the market. Dad was never one to build something that was already available or copy someone else's work—he blazed his own trail. The Power Truck had several features and performance advantages that stood apart in the market. The truck was all-steel welded construction and featured a sliding bed for easy access to the drivetrain, and a flip-over steering wheel for either right or left-hand driving. A front cab-over configuration with front wheel drive/rear wheel steering offered tight turns and easy maneuverability.

While ramping up production of the Power Truck in the early 1960s, a Chicago firm approached Dad with a project for developing and manufacturing a ride-on floor scrubber. The Chicago folks had previously asked another engineering company to convert the Power Truck chassis into a floor scrubber, but the prototype was not working well. They asked Dad to take over. Dad agreed to tackle the project and finished the development of a machine that featured retractable squeegees with hydraulic cylinders, four big front scrubber brushes with hydraulic motors, a vacuum to suck up the water, and two tanks, one for water and chemicals and the other for dirty water.

Over the next few years, we built several dozen machines for the firm. The project nearly came to an end when the company cancelled an order with our money tied up with the work in process. Our attorney advised us to go to court, but instead, Dad took a train to Chicago to hopefully reach a settlement.

I remember Dad describing how big the company was and how small he felt entering the building, almost like crawling on his hands and knees in a beggar's position. The trip paid off, however, and a settlement was reached. But it taught us another valuable lesson. If you are going to do business with a large corporation, in this case performing contract work, remember who is in control. They are!

We continued to build the floor scrubbers, including a larger model Dad designed for the U.S. Navy to scrub aircraft carrier decks. The project gave him the opportunity to travel to Virginia Beach, watch the scrubber being loaded onto the ship's deck, and later test its performance.

Kansas struggles

The hometown bank Dad had been doing business with was familiar with agriculture, but never really understood the financial resources required to manufacture outdoor power equipment like the Power Truck. The bank was always reluctant to give Dad a seasonal line of credit, and it turned down a request to borrow money to fund building the scrubbers for the U.S. Navy, even after Dad showed them the contract.

Eventually, Dad was forced to look for other ways to fund the company. Finding private investors was one potential avenue, but those interested either turned out to be big talkers (the deal was always "next Friday") or demanded control over the company or even part ownership. One prospective investor offered Dad a contract claiming ownership of everything he would develop for the rest of his life. He must have thought Dad was just a hick farmer who was desperate, and someone he could trick.

Although Dad did not finish college because of World War II, and had no formal training in manufacturing, engineering, marketing, or finance, he was no hick farmer. Still, a lack of formal education was likely one reason he eventually retained a professional to manage the company. Seeded with $50,000 in funds Dad borrowed from family, friends, and other small private investors from around the community, that is just what he did.

The first move the new manager made was to lease a new Cadillac. As he told Dad, "You have to look prosperous to be prosperous." He also ordered a big wood desk and other nice furniture to outfit his office while Dad's office featured a single metal desk with a linoleum top. In addition to having expensive tastes, something easy to have when you are spending someone else's money, the new manager had a keen sense of why Dad hired him. He told Dad, "You hired me to do a job, so step aside and let me run the business."

Well, it took more than looking successful to be successful. Dad gave him time to prove himself, but a year and $50,000 later there was nothing to show for it. The company's business position had not changed, and the manager was sent looking for a new job.

That was not the end of the story, however. It took Dad a long time, and likely countless sleepless nights, to pay back the money he owed to his family and friends. I made out a little better. I had graduated from high school the year the manager left, and while running an errand or two for Dad that summer, I was able to look prosperous driving around in that Cadillac.

Move to Casper

To get out from under a growing debt load, Dad figured he would have to sell the Power Truck business, and he did to a Wyoming group looking to diversify beyond its oil and mining operations. The sale paid enough cash for Dad to pay off all his debt prior to leaving Kansas. In 1968, he moved to the new company headquarters in Casper, Wyoming. Once there, however, it was a totally different environment for Dad and my mother. Although they held stock in the company, they had no control. In fact, Dad worked as an employee in product design and development for the new company.

Within two years, a succession of several "professional managers" steered the Power Truck business into bankruptcy. The Wyoming bank not only locked Dad out of the factory, they prevented him access to his tools. After watching professional business managers attempt to operate the company, Dad realized he had a better feel for business and more common sense than they had. He also now had a better understanding of why a family-owned business and being independent was so important to him. Yes, there were risks involved in owning his own business, but the independence would allow him to make his own decisions compared to choosing the easier path of letting someone else manage and fail.

Waiting

There were talks of refinancing and restarting the company, but that never happened. It was not only the end of the Power Truck project, but my parents also lost everything. Dad said we lost everything "except our family and our faith in God." During this time, Dad kept reading his Bible. He said the Scripture messages kept telling him to "wait." That can be a hard message for a man who is used to taking action.

While waiting to see if a restart would be possible, Dad took a $2-an-hour job as a welder for a pre-engineered metal building erection company. One day, while clearing dirt out of a footing for a building foundation, Dad prayed, "Lord, I'm 48 years old. I've worked hard all my life. Is this where I'm supposed to end up?" That very day in 1971 Dad said something arrived in the mail that began to move him to the next opportunity. To this day, I never found out what that "something" was, but sure enough, the opportunity was right around the corner.

Back in business with cab coolers

Next, there came a query from a man in Greeley, Colorado, whom Dad had known from his Kansas days. Hearing that Dad was out of business and working as a welder, he approached him about a project. He asked my dad if he had any interest in developing a new, improved design for a product. The project was for Byco, a sales and marketing firm, and the product was an evaporative tractor cab cooler.

What is an evaporative cooler, you may ask? In hot, dry climates, an evaporative cooler provides cool air as an alternative to refrigeration air conditioning. The evaporative cooler uses a fan to move hot air through a filter pad moistened with water. Natural evaporation causes the air to be cooled (the filter pad also filters out the dust) to make a room, or an enclosure such as a tractor cab, more comfortable on a hot day.

Seeing this as an opportunity to again get involved in design and manufacturing, and regain some independence, Dad agreed to work on the cooler project. To construct the prototype of the cooler, Dad somehow convinced (we are not sure how) the Wyoming bank that had closed and locked up the Power Truck factory to let him back in the building and have access to his tools. Further, when the new cooler design yielded a patent, Mom and Dad sold the design rights to Byco, which gave them enough money to buy back their tools from the bank and open up the factory. Walker began manufacturing tractor cab coolers under contract to Byco in 1972.

As a side note, Dad and Mom always faithfully paid their tithe to the church. Even during this hard time, barely surviving, they wrote the checks to the church and stored them in a dresser drawer. They promised God the checks would be given when the funds became available. Several months later, the checks were delivered.

Encouraged by their early success with cooler production, Dad wanted to move the manufacturing closer to Byco's company headquarters in Greeley.

The move to Fort Collins was made in 1974, where manufacturing was set up in a leased 15,000-sq.-ft. warehouse space on Harmony Road.

A few months later, Dean and I came to work with Dad full-time with our new company that now employed 15 people. For 11 years, from 1972 to 1983, Walker manufactured 70,000 tractor cab coolers and developed new models for recreational vehicles and for residential home use. Throughout, because Byco was our only customer, we were totally dependent on them for cash flow. When they ran into cash flow issues, which they did quite often, we were forced to make "money runs" to Greeley (instead of waiting for their check to arrive in the mail) to make payroll and pay our bills. Speaking of paying bills, with the restart of Walker Manufacturing, Mom resumed her work from her Kansas days, doing the bookkeeping and business office functions. She and Dad were in business together again.

Experimental Projects (1975-1983)

Being totally engaged in the cooler business during much of the '70s didn't stop us from looking for other opportunities. We were restless and had plenty of excess energy to expend in pursuit of other ideas. Part of this drive came from our dependence on Byco, and the fact we did not have a product of our own was of no small concern.

Although the lawn mower was the experiment that eventually became our best opportunity, there were others that we tried:

Quickie Airplane. Dean and I built a kit airplane called the Quickie. It was a single place, tandem wing airplane constructed of moldless foam and fiberglass. It was powered by a 25-hp Onan garden tractor engine and would fly 100 mph. The design originated from the renowned California aircraft designer, Mr. Burt Rutan.

We worked evenings and Saturdays for three years to build the Quickie, and we successfully flew it in the early '80s. We stopped flying it because of some engine vibration problems. At the time, we were also getting busy with the lawn mower project. While it was exciting to fly an airplane built with our own hands, the biggest enjoyment with this project for Dean and me came from working together during the construction phase.

High Mileage Vehicle (HMV). During 1979 and 1980 an oil shortage crisis caused gas prices to double, and they were predicted to go as high as five dollars a gallon. At the time, a fellow in Minnesota was marketing a little one-person car, the HMV (High Mileage Vehicle). His vision, a small, fuel efficient, all-weather vehicle that would get 100 miles per gallon, would be an ideal solution for commuters.

We tried our hand making a vehicle and built two cars from our own three-wheel design, one a rear-wheel and the other a front-wheel drive version. Because of the three-wheel configuration, we eventually licensed one of them as a motorcycle and drove it on the I-25 highway. When we stopped working on the project, the best fuel mileage we achieved was 70 mpg.

Skateboard. In a later chapter, I tell about the skateboard project. While manufacturing coolers, we began to work on putting the skateboard into production. To do that, we updated the design to make the skateboard easier to manufacture. That included making mold patterns to form molded plastic body panels and thinking about ways to market it. A small batch of skateboards was produced and sold.

Feed Bunk. Having a background in farming and ranching, Dad came up with a couple of design ideas for a feed bunk. Typical feed bunks have a smooth bottom panel and allow animals to feed from both sides, a design that often causes animals to fight for access to the feed. Dad's design used a "W" cross-section. The partition in the "W" allowed each animal to feed without competition from the opposing animal.

Dad also designed a modular construction with a "W" sheet metal panel and welded steel leg assemblies. This allowed bunks to be assembled to different sizes just by adding or removing modules. Dad got a patent for the design and produced a few samples. For testing, one of the bunks was sent to my uncle in Kansas who was operating the original Walker farmstead.

CHAPTER 2

Small Beginnings

If you can't buy it, build it, and so we did.

n two ways, the year 1977 happened to be a milestone year for Walker Manufacturing. Both involved turning a dream into reality. When we lived in Kansas, my dad had become a pilot and we had an airplane and airstrip on the family farm. My first airplane ride was with my dad in a 1948 Ryan Navion.

After college, both Dean and I earned our pilot's license and flew rented airplanes on both personal and business trips. In 1977, the dream of owning an airplane came true as the company purchased a brand-new Piper Arrow. Dad and I traveled to the factory in Florida to fly it home. On the way back, a big thunderstorm and hailstorm in Goodland, Kansas, forced us to make an unscheduled stop. While safely on the ground in the terminal building, we watched the hail do its work, putting dents all over our shiny new airplane. Insurance covered the repair of the airplane, and we flew it 1,500 hours over the next several years.

As a young man, I learned that what I had loved, a new shiny airplane, was only a thing. Its real value, dents and all, would come from what it could do for us. Over the next four decades, a company airplane played an important role in helping us develop relationships with our distributor and dealer networks and customers.

Our second hobby (dream) that year was an experiment to see if we could find a better way to mow our lawns. In the spring, Dad and I purchased two riding mowers for use on our half-acre residences in Loveland, Colorado. After a few weeks, we compared notes about how the mowers were working. Both of us had come to the same conclusion: We were disappointed and felt we had made a mistake. Compared to the push mowers we had been using, the riders were not very maneuverable, and it actually took longer to mow the properties with them. Furthermore, the lawns did not look as nice and the grass collection system was not very efficient.

The three of us, Dad, Dean, and myself, put our heads together and decided to try our hand at building a better mower. As we said at the time, "If you can't buy it, build it, and so we did." That slogan has since become part of our company charter to continue to develop new mower models and attachments to better meet the needs of our customers.

The first prototypes

We sold both riding mowers we had purchased earlier and went back to mowing with the walk-behind units we still had. Within a few weeks, Dad and Dean had built the first prototype Walker Mower. By summertime we were mowing our properties with our new design. Right from the start, the prototype mower was working better than the riding mowers we had purchased. Unbeknownst to us, our journey had begun. We built two more prototypes, one in 1978 and another in 1979, each one improving on what we had learned. The last prototype became the pattern for the first 25 machines produced in 1980.

At the time, we had not developed a long-term strategy to get into the lawn mower business. This was a hobby, an experiment, to find a better way to mow our properties. Even though manufacturing coolers was paying our bills, something told us our new design had business potential.

In 1979, to gauge the interest farmers might have in our machine (since farmers are a good judge of equipment), we took our third prototype to a farm show in Great Bend, Kansas. There we discovered not only interest in our mower, but also a level of disappointment among some farmers that we had nothing to sell to them. That was all the encouragement we needed, and upon returning home, we made plans to produce 25 machines the following year.

With little tooling and a lot of hand building, it took us one year to build 25 machines. Since we had no distributors or dealers, selling those first 25 mowers took two years.

Marketing lesson

From our earlier experiences with the golf car and Power Truck, and with Byco cooler products, we learned that if a company wanted to control its destiny, it had to be in control of not only the manufacturing process, but the marketing of its products, as well. Leaving marketing to a third party essentially relegated the manufacturer to the back seat.

With our new lawn mower, we were determined to stay in the front seat, to do both the manufacturing and the marketing. This was a challenge at first. We did not consider ourselves to be marketers and, furthermore, we had little marketing experience.

We forged ahead, developing advertising material and brochures. To kickstart our marketing, we ran "new product" press releases in 25 industry publications. An inventor we knew suggested we use press releases because they are run at no cost by the publication. As the inventor instructed, I went to the Colorado State University (CSU) library and used a big book of USA periodicals to make a list of publications whose readers I thought would have an interest in a new lawn mower. That list became our mailing list to the publications.

In 1981, Mom and Dad took several laps around the country, demonstrating the mower to readers who had responded to the releases. The trips accumulated orders for 100 machines with 10 percent money down for security.

At one 24-hour stop in Florida, the very first inquiry was from a Sarasota landscape maintenance company that gave us a money-down order for 48 machines (remember we had made only 25 machines so far), and they signed on to be our first dealer/distributor. The company owner told us this was just the machine he had been looking for to mow the small plots of grass around some of the millions of retirement homes in the state.

When Dad phoned home, I asked about the short stay in Florida. He told me that in addition to placing the order, the Sarasota company bought everything, including the demonstrator machine and the trailer they used to tow it around on. So, they fired up their 1974 Chevy Blazer and were headed home.

In 1982, we manufactured 125 Walker Mowers, 100 of which were pre-sold, and the remainder built on speculation. This was a slow start and a small beginning for us. The slow start turned out to be a good thing. Among several improvements we made early on, we discovered in Florida that our mower blades were turning too slowly to cut the grass cleanly. We were easily able to correct this and make other improvements since we had only a few units in the field.

Toward independence

A recession in the early 1980s was especially hard on the agricultural market. With many of its cooler products designed for use on farm tractors, Byco suffered along with other companies in the industry, and they began to look for a buyer or business partner. They found a new business partner who, in turn, inquired if we had any desire to merge with them. The partner likely expected Dad to jump at the chance to grow with the company. Instead, he reiterated our goal to stay independent.

A little later, Byco attempted to sell the cooler project, the coolers we made, to another company.

An acquisition man from that company paid us a visit to determine our interest in being part of the sale. He told us that if we did not sell the company to them it would "blow the deal." Worse yet, he threatened us by telling us if we did not agree to be part of the sale, "You have built your last cooler."

Even while knowing that manufacturing coolers was our bread and butter, we did not think twice about our response. We were going to remain independent. In the fall of 1983, Byco announced they were taking the coolers from us and moving the manufacturing of them to their facility in Greeley, Colorado. They had the perfect right to do so since we had sold them the patent, design rights, and tooling many years earlier.

Under our arrangement with Byco, they owned the material and we converted the material to a finished product for a contracted price. Upon taking back the cooler business, the company still owed us for $120,000 of work in process. Despite a bank guarantee that was about to expire, Byco management gave Dad their word they would pay us. Dad let the bank guarantee expire and in a direct violation of their word, Byco did not pay us. On the advice of our attorney we locked up the finished product. Byco then took us to court and the judge awarded us $60,000 or 50 cents on the dollar.

The court's decision was a huge loss for a small company like ours trying to get into the lawn mower business. We needed the cash Byco owed us for the work in process to help pay expenses and survive while we worked on our new project. Dad had trusted their word and they broke it. I felt like Byco had their hands around our throat choking us to death. I hated Byco for what they had done.

Forgiveness is often a process. Over time, with the Lord's help, I was able to forgive and get peace in my heart. I never forgot, but there was sweet peace. A year or so later, I was traveling and happened to see one of the Byco partners at a filling station in southern Colorado. He warily approached me, and in asking for my forgiveness said, "The way we treated you was wrong." I was happy to tell him I had forgiven him a long time ago.

Best opportunity

There was no other way to describe it. Losing the Byco cooler business, something we had been doing for 11 years, was a huge loss, not to mention the $60,000 hit we took at the end. We had worked hard and poured our lives and energy into the design and manufacturing of the cooler. However, looking back, it was God's hand at work as He was moving us toward our best opportunity, to develop the Walker Mower.

In fact, we could not have timed it better to get into the mower business. Along with several other smaller companies, we were introducing zero-turn mowers into the marketplace at the beginning of a new, beneficial trend in mower design. It would be another 15 years before major manufacturers would begin to produce similar mowers. In the meantime, we would be getting our brand established in the market.

What we also did not know at the time was cab coolers for tractors were gradually being replaced by factory-installed refrigerated air conditioning units. The market for cab coolers and our relationship with Byco would have lasted only a few more years anyway.

In 1984, without the coolers, we were committed to go full-time into the lawn mower business. It was either that or go out of business. That year, we made and sold 450 machines and got paid for every one of them. Still, on paper, we were nearly broke (again). We simply did not have enough cash flow to buy materials, pay the labor and overhead expenses, convert to finished product, and get the cash back several times in 12 months. I always tell people it was a miracle that we made it. But we did, and we know where the help came from. During this time, we never thought or talked about the possibility of failure.

From the time we built our first prototype mower, it would take us 10 years to make a profit manufacturing our zero-turn mowers. That may seem unbelievably long, but it takes a long time to build a good reputation for your product and brand name. Even having a lot of money does not necessarily accelerate the brand-building process.

CHAPTER 3

Building Blocks

*The most interesting part of making lawn
mowers is the stories told by our customers as
they put their mowers to work. This puts the
emphasis where it should be, on people.*

My dad always wanted to own the land and
the building for his factory as he did when
we lived in Fowler, Kansas, and it took
us 15 years leasing space in Fort Collins for that to
happen. He was constantly looking for a place to
build. Many looked promising, but obstacles such
as utilities, zoning, and lack of infrastructure were in
the way. Being in the lawn mower business, we were

also looking for some acreage with water wells so we could grow grass for test mowing.

Finally, a 50-acre tract of land with two good irrigation wells became available. Coincidentally, the land was still on Harmony Road but located in a rural area east of Fort Collins. One of the first obstacles to overcome was rezoning the farmland. Our attorney initially thought it would take approximately six months and $25,000 to have the property rezoned. Instead, it took more than twice that long at double the cost. There were other roadblocks such as financing and having enough water flow for the fire protection system, each with the potential to stop us. One by one, though, we overcame them. In May 1990, the new building, a 76,000-sq.- ft. structure with 16,000 sq. ft. of office space and 60,000 sq. ft. for the factory floor was completed, and we moved in.

It took 49 semi-truck loads to move us. Since it was springtime, we could not afford to shut down manufacturing. By phasing the move over a couple of weeks, it allowed us to retain our full production schedule.

For my dad, the factory felt like home in more ways than one. He always believed in living close to work. Our Kansas farmhouse had been right next to the factory. At our new factory in Fort Collins, right from the start we designed a 4,000-sq.-ft. apartment upstairs for my folks. It was finished as beautifully as any custom-built home would be, and it had an especially nice feature for Dad. A window in the living area offered a bird's-eye view of the factory floor below. Mom and Dad lived there, as close as one could get to the production line, for the rest of their lives. The apartment has since been reconfigured into an expanded office area, but we retain wonderful memories of this space when it was an apartment.

We dedicated the new building and land to the Lord and invited our employees, our church family, and pastor to come join us for dedication. Today, when visitors come to visit our factory, they stand on dedicated ground, a piece of land for which we have found many wonderful uses. In addition to test mowing, we hold outdoor celebrations, an annual Hymn Sing, and sales training events there. We also have a beautiful grass airstrip to take off and land our small airplanes.

You may be wondering, what is a Hymn Sing? Many churches today have stopped singing the historic hymns, replacing them with a new style of worship music. In 2004, we got the vision to invite our neighbors from all across northern Colorado to gather on our lawn and sing 24 traditional hymns. Walker sponsors this gathering (it is not sponsored by a church and nothing is charged for attending). Now, for the last 16 years, every June we have had more than 1,000 neighbors come and sing and worship God with us. Imagine singing "How Great Thou Art" with 1,000 other people with the backdrop of the majestic Rockies on a beautiful evening in June and you have the idea.

Building a market

As mentioned earlier, when we started selling mowers, our vision for the future did not extend far beyond Colorado and a few neighboring states. Within the next eight years we would develop a large distribution network throughout North America, Europe, Australia, New Zealand, and South Africa. How did we accomplish that? Out of the millions of people around the world who would have offered to help us, how did we find the right ones to work with? As people of faith, we would answer it was not blind luck or chance meetings. Rather, it was good providence from the hand of our Creator.

Our first export opportunity to Australia in 1984 illustrates how our network was assembled. The story begins when an individual named John Stead from Wagga Wagga, New South Wales, Australia, (approximately a four-and-a-half-hour drive south of Sydney) called us. He had seen a small postage-stamp-size advertisement we had placed in *Implement & Tractor* magazine. The advertisement was simply a picture of our mower, yet it was enough to pique his curiosity.

At the time, John was already importing farm machinery from North America. He told me he would like to order a sample machine. Having no experience in exporting, I asked him how he would pay for it and he said, "I will wire you the money." That sounded good to me, and I agreed to send him a machine.

A month or so later, John called and informed me he would like to order a container load (valued around $100,000 USD). Again, I asked about payment and he said he would pay half now and send the balance when we were ready to ship. We agreed to that arrangement, but a couple of weeks before we were ready to ship the units, our bank informed us that the other half of the funds were already in our account. The man from Australia trusted us completely, and we continue to work with him and his family to this day. The Steads now have a third-generation family member working in their company.

That, however, is not the end of the story. John introduced us to his friends in New Zealand, South Africa, and British Columbia, Canada. Collectively, the sales of thousands upon thousands of machines can be traced to the small magazine advertisement and that first phone call from him.

We met other pioneering Walker Mower distributors either at trade shows or from press releases, editorials, or small advertisements we ran in trade publications. Among them were Bob Oestreich, Port Washington, New York, (Northeastern USA); Sven Gillfors, Malmo, Sweden (Europe); and Percy Schneider, Ontario, Canada (Eastern Canada). All made significant contributions introducing Walker Mowers into their markets.

Thinking back, I recall a rather funny incident

that occurred between one of the above pioneers, Bob Oestreich, and my dad. In the fall of 1982, we went to our first trade show that was east of the Mississippi, the Garden Industry of America (GIA) show held in Cincinnati, Ohio. Since we were a "first-timer," we had no priority on our booth location and found ourselves off the main floor and back in the corner of the upper mezzanine.

Despite our location, we were excited about being there. But during the first hours of the show, attendees showed little interest and walked right on by our booth with one little Walker Mower on display. Then, seemingly out of nowhere, a man walked up, stopped, and looked at the mower. "This is just what I've been looking for," he said. The individual happened to be Bob Oestreich, and he had a "bigger than life personality" with a New York accent to boot.

He told me and my dad he wanted to take the machine home, try it out, and see if it would cut and catch grass in New York. If it did, he would consider being a distributor for us.

He then informed us that a death in his family required him to leave the show early and return to New York. My dad asked about payment for the machine, and Bob told him that a Connecticut friend of his was also exhibiting at the show. He could transport the mower to New York for him and would write Dad a check. Bob apparently did not have a check on him.

Before the show ended, my dad visited Bob's friend to make the transportation arrangements. When my dad asked for the check, the Connecticut friend became angry, fighting mad angry. He was insulted that we would not trust his friend to pay us. My dad backed away and let the mower go without a check. That was hard to do since we were in no position to lose the price of the mower.

Yes, Bob Oestreich paid us for the mower. It worked just fine in New York and the rest is history. Bob introduced the Walker Mower to eight states in the Northeast and became our largest distributor.

Similar to the other stories about coming across the one person we needed to meet, in 1985 we met Mr. Sven Gillfors from Malmo, Sweden, at the Power Equipment EXPO in Louisville, Kentucky. He was a gentle giant of a man. When we met him, Sven was a manufacturer's representative in Europe working with a couple other American power equipment manufacturers. He immediately was interested in working with us to introduce the Walker to Europe.

He had a lot of knowledge and experience with outdoor power equipment in the European market. With Sven leading the way, Walker premiered in 1986 at the GAFA show in Cologne, Germany. Today, thousands of Walker Mowers have been sent to the European market growing out of meeting Mr. Gillfors.

Walker Talk magazine

In 1992, I received a magazine from Beechcraft Aircraft Corporation presumably because I was a private pilot and on the company's mailing list. The magazine shared stories about how Beechcraft airplanes were being used to impact and improve the lives of its readers/customers. The approach intrigued me. I called the magazine's publishing company and mentioned we would be interested in producing a similar publication about how customers were using our zero-turn mowers, and *Walker Talk* magazine was born.

The first issue was mailed in July 1992, and

over the next 28 years, 56 regular issues and three special editions (two for Australasia and one for Europe) have been published and 2,750,000 copies distributed. Throughout, hundreds of customers from all over the world have been interviewed, and we have told their stories.

We have always believed the most interesting part of making lawn mowers is the stories told by our customers as they put the mowers to work. This puts the emphasis where it should be, on people. This approach is how we like to operate, "family-style," in contrast to how most big corporate manufacturers operate.

All the *Walker Talk* stories have been created by going on-site, which means our editor, Rod Dickens, has traveled around the world interviewing customers face-to-face and taking photographs. The main reason for traveling, in lieu of conducting phone interviews, is to ensure the stories will be authentic. We wanted the editor to get to know the customer and find out for himself how the mower or mowers were used. Customers were always encouraged to avoid staging or using other forms of manipulation that would take the story out of context. We simply want the truth to be told about our product in real world use.

Of course, the temptation to put the best foot forward is hard to resist, especially when your business is going to appear in a publication. Rod told me of one occasion when a contractor, posing for a photo shoot on his mower, nearly slipped off the seat. He looked at Rod sheepishly and simply said, "I told my employee to spray Armor All® on the tires, not the seat, too!"

Speaking of truth-telling about our products, we have always avoided using paid endorsements or a paid spokesperson for the Walker Mower. Over the years numerous customers, even a few celebrities, have offered to promote the mower for receiving compensation. We have stayed away from that approach simply because we want our customers to tell the truth about the mower, both the good stories and even those that were not so good. Even the most ethical individuals who are paid to endorse a product often find it hard to tell the truth.

Walker Talk is still alive and interesting as a publication because our vision with the magazine has been to go beyond selling a machine to inspiring, encouraging, and uplifting our customers and potential customers. It is exciting to read about young people starting in business, middle-aged entrepreneurs having a business of their own, elderly people making extra income, those with dual careers advancing, women in business, award-winning private gardeners, small companies and big companies, all sharing their use of the little yellow machines. We have been careful not to make the machine the main part of the story; it's not the machine, it is what the machine does that makes the difference in the story.

Celebrating

We believe bringing all sorts of people together to celebrate an occasion, accomplishment, or special event helps to forge a family-like bond. I have always admired what Harley Davidson has done, bringing together owners of their products. It does not matter if you are white, black, brown, blue collar, white collar, man, or woman, if you ride a Harley you are in a club where barriers come down and everyone is equal and standing on level ground.

We are not nearly as big as Harley or as well

known, but on a smaller scale our company has brought people together for a Walker Family Reunion. Held at the factory, the three get-togethers so far have celebrated reaching important milestones, the production of mower number 50,000, 100,000, and 150,000. Thousands of people from all over the world who have interest in our little yellow mowers, including factory employees, suppliers, distributors, dealers, and our end-customers, have celebrated with us.

The family-style approach to business creates a special camaraderie where people enjoy being part of something where they are appreciated, where there is a relationship and interest in people that goes beyond the mechanics of selling equipment and taking money from customers. It is hard to believe, but there really are Walker Mower enthusiasts who love being right in the middle of a gathering of other Walker people. Products from most big corporations do not share in this appeal.

It takes tremendous organization, time, and resources to put together a celebration like the Walker Family Reunion. Assuredly, budget watchers for larger corporations would say it is not worth the time, energy, and cost. But that is one of several advantages of being a private, family-owned company. We are accountable to ourselves, and for us, loving our Walker Mower family and celebrating with them is well worth it.

At Walker Manufacturing, getting together with factory employees is something we do throughout the year to celebrate anniversaries, special events, and reaching goals. The latter are "parties with a purpose," the result of setting and reaching a goal, and goal setting is a vital company activity. Without goals a company will perish.

These celebrations also energize people to set and reach new goals, to start the next cycle (what is our next goal?). They reinforce teamwork where individuals recognize their part in reaching company goals and realize they were able to accomplish more for themselves by working together as part of a company versus working individually.

One celebration I have with employees is to take them out for lunch at a restaurant of their choice on their fifth anniversary. This gives me an opportunity to get better acquainted with employees, hear their stories, and thank them for their good work in the company. There have been 281 lunches since we started doing them in the early '90s. When I ask employees how they first heard about the company and the opportunity at Walker Manufacturing, they usually point to a referral from a family member, friend, or neighbor as the source.

We have other parties for our employees and their families (kids included). A company picnic in the summer and the annual Christmas party are opportunities to bring our people together and deepen our relationships. Finally, each month on a Friday afternoon, we have a "shop meeting" (on the time clock). We stop working 30 minutes early and gather in our lunchroom/meeting room where there's space for everyone to be seated, and snacks and drinks are served.

Here, I give a "State of the Company" report to let everyone know how the company is doing and where the company is headed in the days ahead. At this meeting, we take time for questions and answers. We also celebrate employee employment anniversaries at 20-plus years. Occasionally we invite a customer to come into the meeting, stand up in front of the whole company, and give their testimonial on the impact of the Walker Mower in their life. Communicating and celebrating with employees is an essential way to help keep everybody "in the know" and enthused.

Dan Walker, loss

A few days before our second Family Reunion Celebration in July 2008, my nephew, Dean's third-oldest son, Dan, passed away in his sleep from a ruptured aortic aneurysm. He had graduated in the spring with a degree in mechanical engineering from Olivet Nazarene University in Illinois and was working that summer as a counselor at a Christian summer camp. His passing was a tremendous shock and blow to our immediate family. Even as we were grieving, the decision was made to go ahead with the celebration.

There is no explanation or words to make any sense of the loss of a young person. Dan had so much talent and passion for life, and we were looking forward to seeing if he would become another third-generation family member to work in the Walker Manufacturing Company. We could tell he had a special gift like Dean and his grandfather to design and build machines. While we will never understand, we are optimistic people and will leave this all in God's hands. He numbers all our days.

Our family

A lot of this story revolves around my dad. But as has often been said, behind every successful man is a great woman. That was my mom. My two sisters, Ruth and Nina, and my brother Dean and I, were raised by two parents who loved each other and loved us. What a privilege to grow up this way. We experienced a real upbringing and much of that credit goes to Mom.

Mom was a woman of faith. She knew her God and believed. Most all the stories in the Bible I first heard from my mom reading them to me. She believed the stories and so did I.

Mom knew courage, every bit as much as my dad. I never heard anything from her but "move ahead" when the decision was made to start the manufacturing company. Mom shared the dream and was Dad's companion in business right from the start. Even when the business failed in Casper, Wyoming, and had to be started all over again, Mom was the optimist, and her faith was intact. Mom and Dad were two strands of a cord that would not be broken.

Mom knew who she was. She was an old-fashioned woman of grace, graciousness, and dignity. She was also a modern woman who could think for herself and, at the same time, respectfully join forces with my dad. I never heard them argue and I never heard her say anything disparaging about my dad. I do know that she sometimes disagreed with Dad, but with civility.

Mom and Dad were musicians. She was a talented pianist and organist, and Dad played the stand-up string bass. They would sing specials in church and revival services. A favorite memory as kids is falling asleep hearing our parents singing together and playing their instruments. Music was a big part of our family's home life.

CHAPTER 4

In Search of Perfection

*In the quest for perfection, many of our deck
designs have evolved with two, three, or four
deck configurations since first introduced.*

F orty-three years after designing our first lawn
mower, one would think we have the perfect
machine and are ready to move on to the
next project. Instead, we continue to work every
day on improving our machine's design. Whereas
many engineers want to design something and then
move on to design something else, Dean is fascinated
by designing a machine to its highest possible
performance level, and he has the persistence and

discipline to carry it through.

This approach is not as glamorous as designing, building, and always bringing new products to the marketplace, but it is substantial and helps us stay ahead of competitors large and small alike. Our products must have irresistible superiority in both design and performance and in uncompromising quality to be successful in the market. We could not survive with "average" products in the market with big competitors.

Our "Walker Product Philosophy" statement developed in the '80s says it very well: "The only way for a small company to enter an established market and stay there is to design products with irresistible superiority and uncompromising quality. A conventional product with conventional performance may be acceptable and even attractive when offered by a large established company; the same product offered by a small company cannot hope to survive in the marketplace where profit margins are small, competition is strong, and consumer loyalty to existing product lines is great."

A few years after marketing the Walker Mower, we had requests from customers and dealers to build a larger, scaled-up version. We started to work constructing a prototype, and then one day we woke up and realized that we needed to make some improvements for our machine currently on the market.

It would have been a big mistake to lose our focus on the current mower model in pursuit of the bigger machine. We put the bigger machine on the shelf and never looked back. Incidentally, we believe we could have built a bigger machine that could have been successful in the market, but it would not be worth it at the cost of possibly losing the opportunity with the machine that was currently on the market.

Our small size gave us the flexibility to stay focused on improving our product. It also gave us the competitive advantage of being agile and making improvements quickly. Bigger companies simply cannot move as fast. Across the years, we have made hundreds of improvements to our mowers and have often introduced running changes on the production line rather than waiting for a model year.

We also quickly adopted new technology when it became available. For example, when the V-twin engine was introduced in the early '90s, we quickly integrated it into our basic design, packing 20-hp into the chassis that was originally sized for an 11-

hp, single-cylinder engine. We were early adopters of electronic fuel injection on the engines used in our mowers, offering increased fuel economy and better engine performance. It would be 10 years or so before some of the big companies would introduce electronic fuel injection into their lineup.

Deck discipline

Designing mower decks to accommodate multiple mowing conditions and grass types requires more than looking at some engineering drawings and making a few changes. Instead, from our perspective, nothing beats good old-fashioned trial and error. To that point, my brother (and Dad) have made literally thousands of adjustments to the deck housing, blades, and baffles to find the right configuration for a deck to deliver a beautiful cut, be clog-resistant, and handle clippings well.

The design must also work equally well in all types of grass, climates, and preferred cutting heights that vary from different regions within this country and from others around the world. In the quest for perfection, many of our deck designs have evolved with two, three, or four design configurations since first introduced.

In other words, it takes a long time to go from having a good idea to making and marketing a great product, and who is to say which of the three requisites are most important? They are all needed to be successful. What is also true is it requires discipline and focus to select the best ideas, the ones that have the biggest market potential.

We are grateful for having our share of successful "light bulb" moments over the years, but we also know that we do not hold a monopoly on them. Surely, we have been the beneficiary of listening to customers and others regarding ways to improve our product. It has been surprising, as well, to see all the attachments and accessories for our Walker Mowers developed by others, some with great success and others with more narrow appeal.

Less surprising is seeing the number of manufacturers that have tried to run with our original design, to develop small, maneuverable mowers that deliver an excellent cut and overall performance. Some would say copying one's idea is the highest form of flattery. We say that it takes more than a good idea, even a great one that is borrowed, to produce a great product.

Even as a number of manufacturers were copying our design, naysayers were predicting no lasting future for our product or our company. Before the zero-turn and steering lever style riding mower became popular in the mid-1990s one of the larger companies whose mowers had steering wheels commissioned a market study on the acceptance of steering levers. They told us that steering levers were a fad that would never become popular and we should redesign our mowers to use steering wheels. How wrong they were. In today's market, steering levers are used on 98 to 99 percent of commercial riding mowers.

Several years ago, another study conducted by a major lawn mower manufacturer predicted that within five to 10 years the lawn mower manufacturing industry would consolidate into five companies and Walker was not on the list. Guess what? We are still here, the Walker Mower is still here, and we are determined to be here for years to come.

Trial and error

Another benefit to using trial and error discipline is the "error" can lead to discoveries that further lead to other opportunities. In the early 2000s, we got the idea to make a walk-behind tractor that would use the same mower deck attachments as our riding mowers; we thought there would be a new market for us to enter with the walk-behind. After several years, we had produced and sold a few hundred walk-behinds, but the market never developed as we envisioned, and we discontinued the unit.

A big mistake? In developing the walk-behind, we used a new hydrostatic transaxle for the ground drive and discovered this component worked very well. That led us to develop a new riding tractor using the new transaxle, the Model B, which has become a very important part of our product line since being introduced in 2004. The discoveries made while working with the walk-behind design (which failed) became the steppingstone to a new, successful addition to our product line.

CHAPTER 5

Preparing Family Leaders

*I remember very well the day that Dad walked
into my office that year and said, "I want you to
start signing as president of the company."*

I f a family business is to continue into the next
generation, those family members who wish to
participate in the business will need to prepare
ahead of time. There is no set time when this
preparation begins or what path it will take. The
process itself is as varied and as unique as we all
are uniquely created. One important principle to
remember is to avoid putting pressure on family
members to join the company or to take the rather

extreme approach and say to them, "You must join the family business."

Joining the family business should be their decision entirely, with one prerequisite: Each person needs to have the passion, interest, talent, and giftedness to help the business move forward. With all it takes to operate a business, the company should not be left to those family members who have only a half-hearted interest in its success or who are focused on the wrong things such as thinking the business is primarily a "money multiplier" or a "money spout" for individual pursuits.

Ideally, family members will have a significant amount of time to prepare and take on additional responsibilities. Unfortunately, sometimes a catastrophic situation such as poor health or a divorce can suddenly disable the current family business leader and thrust the next generation into a leadership position without the necessary experience, training, and preparation. Tragically, businesses that encounter these circumstances often fail.

Max Walker Family in the mid-1950s
(L to R) Dean, Ruth, Margaret, Max, Nina, Bob

Walker family farm, Fowler, Kansas, circa 1950s
before manufacturing building was constructed

Dad with Allis Chalmers crawler
tractor used for farming

Dean pushing dirt with miniature bulldozer

*Exhibiting golf car and bulldozer at the
Kansas State Fair in Hutchinson, Kansas*

Golf cars production started in old farm shop in 1957

Golf cars lined up in front of first factory building

*Max with the Walker Executive
golf car at a country club*

Walker Power Truck in early 60s

*Dean seated on sixty-inch floor scrubber designed
and manufactured for a Chicago company*

*Aircraft carrier deck scrubber built
on contract for the US Navy*

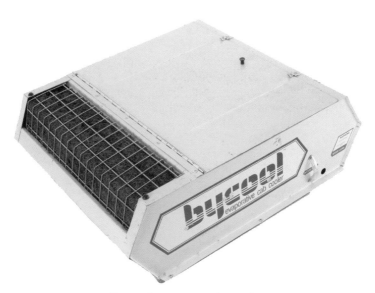

Bycool tractor cab cooler

Dean tests first mower prototype (1977)

Max and Margaret making early exhibit of Walker Mowers at the Kansas 3I Farm Show in '80 or '81. In the background is the Chevy Blazer they used to tour the USA making demonstrations.

Celebrating production of the 10,000th Walker
Mower in 1991 (L to R) Dean, Margaret, Max, Bob

*Walker Mowers are in use around the world,
shown here at Westminster Abbey, London, UK*

Walker men posing for a promotional photo in 2004

Fifty-six issues of Walker Talk
magazine published since 1992

Walker Family Reunion II celebrating the 100,000th Walker Mower in August 2008. Approximately 2,300 guests attended the two-day event

Navigating hay bales on the skateboard

Walker factory sits on 61 acres with lots of grass for test mowing (2018)

Second- and third-generation Walkers look to the future (L to R) Ted, Dean, Bob, Ryan

Hymn Sing on factory grounds

Learning curve

Even though Dad had been used to calling all the shots when Dean and I began working with him, he very gracefully let us take on more responsibility and decision making. This gave us an incredible opportunity to prepare for the day when we would assume control.

Dean and I joined the business in 1975, and Dad handed over leadership to us in 1990. I remember very well the day that Dad walked into my office that year and said, "I want you to start signing as president of the company." I had neither asked for this position nor had I even thought about it—it was all Dad's initiative. I also remember that the next day did not feel any different from the day before. I had already been doing the work and taking the responsibilities of the president. The title made no difference. In 2001, Dad had a stroke that ended his days of being active in the business.

Dean and I began preparing long before we assumed leadership in Walker Manufacturing. It began when we were young boys growing up in the business. I recall that after school, the bus would drop us off and we would quickly change clothes and head out to the shop. Homework could wait until the next morning.

It was during this time that Dad taught us how to work in the manufacturing business. We learned arc welding, machining, metal working, painting, and assembly. Also, when Dad was conducting a business meeting, he would invite us to sit in and listen to the conversation. There was one rule: don't talk, just listen. Right from the very start, Dean and I loved the manufacturing business. Here we are 60-plus years later still enjoying designing, making, and selling machines.

Different paths

Dean and I took quite different paths for our preparation. When I was 12 or 13, our family heard Mr. R.G. LeTourneau speak at a gathering in Ashland, Kansas. LeTourneau was the inventor of large earth-moving equipment, and he flew around the country telling his story about how the Lord had blessed him. My parents were inspired by reading LeTourneau's book, *Mover of Men and Mountains*, and we went to hear him speak.

The part of his talk that resonated most with me was when he told about meeting with his minister after dedicating himself to living for the Lord. He had prayed to the Lord, "I will do anything You want me to do from this day on." He assumed that would mean he would need to stop being a businessman and become a minister or full-time Christian worker. But his minister said, "God needs businessmen as well as preachers and missionaries." At that moment, I realized that was what the Lord had in store for me to do.

I began to follow the path to become a Christian businessman. This included getting a mechanical engineering degree at LeTourneau College (now LeTourneau University) in Longview, Texas, an institution founded by Mr. LeTourneau. After graduating in 1969, there was no opportunity to join Walker Manufacturing since the company had been sold. At the time, the Vietnam War was in full swing and it was fairly certain I would be drafted after completing college. If I were to serve, I wanted to have the chance to fly airplanes. So, I tried to enlist in the Air Force, but didn't pass the physical. The flight surgeon told me I would never be able to fly because of a skin condition on my hands (long since resolved). Instead, I accepted a job offer from Cessna Aircraft Company in Wichita, Kansas, to work as a structural engineer in their military aircraft program. The position included a draft deferment that allowed me to put my engineering degree to work in an area where I enjoyed working, with aircraft.

I spent six years at Cessna, advancing to become an engineering group leader. Many of the lessons and operating principles learned at Cessna helped me after joining the family business. In addition to getting some leadership experience, it taught me that family-run businesses and large companies like Cessna have many of the same challenges to overcome. To be sure, working outside the family business gave me an important perspective that would prove invaluable.

Dean, Ted, and Ryan

Dean started his preparation to lead the company when he was in junior high. With access to the shop tools, materials, and components, he began to design and build all kinds of machines, including the powered sit-down skateboards and go-karts. From my observation, Dean inherited a magnificent giftedness from Dad to put together machines, maybe showing an even stronger gift. He continued to develop his skills and hone his art with a hands-on approach with no formal education in engineering; more important, he had our dad as his teacher.

Dean attended junior college close to home his first two years. He took time off in the second semester of his sophomore year to help Dad build the tooling for manufacturing the Byco evaporative cooler. In 1975, he graduated from Northwest Nazarene College (now Northwest Nazarene University) in Nampa, Idaho, with a degree in business administration and immediately came to work at Walker Manufacturing.

My brother's only job has been working with Walker Manufacturing for 45 years. Many family businesses have a rule that family members need to have experience working for another company before joining the family business. This has proven to be a good, common sense rule. For every rule, though, there is an exception; Dean's experience is that exception. As it turned out, a couple of years after joining the company, Dean's skills were needed to help build the first Walker Mower prototype.

Dean's two oldest sons, Ted and Ryan, also took their own unique paths to Walker Manufacturing. Following that common sense rule mentioned above, we encouraged them to have some experience working in another company before joining the family business.

Ted graduated from Olivet Nazarene University in Kankakee, Illinois, with a degree in mechanical engineering. His first job was with a civil engineering firm in Kankakee. Soon after joining the company, he met a girl from Idaho whom he eventually married (quite often there is a girl in the story) and took a job at Eagle R&D in Caldwell, Idaho.

Eagle produced the kit-built Helicycle helicopter. Ted worked at Eagle for six years and was involved in producing batches of parts for the helicopter and assembling the kits. During his Idaho tenure, he started working part-time for Walker in compliance engineering. After eight years of experience elsewhere, Ted moved to Colorado and came to work full-time in the family business.

Ryan, too, graduated from Olivet, but with a degree in business administration. He pursued additional training at the School of Missionary Aviation Technology in Lowell, Michigan, where he obtained both his Airframe & Powerplant Mechanics license and his Commercial and Certified Flight Instructor-Instrument (CFII) airplane pilot's license.

Before joining Walker Manufacturing, Ryan and his wife, Emily, contracted with the SEND mission organization to live for three years in the Cup'ik Alaska native village of Chevak. There, on the Alaskan western frontier, the couple taught school, Ryan flew for missions, and they worked with the local church.

The village has a population of 900 and is accessible only by air or snow machine. In fact, the nearest road is 500 miles away. In an aviation course Ryan taught for junior high and high school students, one project was for students to help him build a kit airplane, a RANS S-6. At the end of the three-year commitment with SEND, Ryan flew the airplane 2,700 miles home to Colorado and came to work with Walker Manufacturing.

Despite all the different paths and preparation the second and third generation family members took to assume leadership roles, nothing was probably more important than sharing experiences once working within the company. Dean and I, for example, developed a habit early on to have lunch with Dad every day. During the hour, we talked about a lot of different things, but business was always on the agenda. Dad was an amazing man with a strong work ethic, lots of common sense, and years of experience. We could not help but walk away from those lunches being better prepared to run the company. We've continued the tradition with Ted and Ryan. Every Tuesday, the four of us eat breakfast together off-site.

Hand-off

Like many business owners, my parents dreamed of keeping the business ownership and management within their family and remaining independent. My brother Dean and I have worked diligently to make that possible by creating a generational transfer (business succession) plan. The planning work started when I was 56 years old. Why so early? The earlier the planning starts, the more options that become available. Put another way, options diminish over time, and along with them, so does the plan. Having the time to mentor generation leaders is another good reason to get started early.

To paraphrase business management consultant Peter Drucker, the final test of a good leader is how well he chooses his successor and whether he can step aside to let his successor take his place. A good leader will work and plan for his successor to be even more successful than he has been. Dad understood this and was a great model for Dean and me. I don't think stepping aside was easy for Dad, nor is it for most entrepreneurs, but he did what was right for the future of the business.

After completing a 10-year leadership training program administered by an outside consultant, Ted and Ryan are beginning to take over the reins of operating the company, just as my dad did for Dean and me in 1990. The transfer began officially in 2019 when Ryan became company President and Ted became Vice President of Engineering.

The succession plan also involves a financial ownership transfer, giving financial control to Ryan and Ted while providing Dean and me and our wives financial security for the rest of our lives. We believe that keeping ownership within our family also helps secure the future of all those who are invested in our company: employees, suppliers, distributors, dealers, and end-customers. Ryan and Ted have a younger brother, Kyle, who is currently working as a sales representative for Walker Distributing Company (a subsidiary of Walker Manufacturing) in Kentucky and Tennessee. Sometime in the future, he too may join our company in a leadership position.

Dad always taught us that family members who are active in managing the family business should have financial control. Similarly, the stock in the company needs to be concentrated in the hands of those family members who are making the business go forward. If too much of the ownership has been gifted or distributed to too many family members, then family business managers can lose control and it becomes a recipe for disaster. Family members not active in managing the business have a whole different perspective about what it means to own stock in the business.

Dad and Mom worked for several years on a plan to transition the company ownership and control to Dean and me. In earlier years, all of us siblings had been gifted equal amounts of stock, but in the late 1980s, Dean and I were gifted enough stock to have control (our parents took a minority stock position), and our two sisters received an equivalent amount of cash, based on the current valuation of the company. My parents were willing to sacrifice their hard-won "ownership" and take the necessary steps for the family control to go to the next generation. At the same time, they showed their love and care for my sisters who were not active in the business.

An attitude of entitlement by any family member working in a family business is destructive and deadly to the company's future. It cannot be tolerated and must be identified and removed. You do not want to sacrifice the business for your family or your family for your business, a delicate balance for most family businesses.

CHAPTER 6

The Great Recession

You do not know the strength of your
relationships until tested in a hard time.

After 30-plus years of making a profit, the economic recession in 2009 hit us hard. Springtime sales dried up, and we began to lose a lot of money. At the time, we were experiencing a double whammy. In addition to the recession, we were dealing with an expensive warranty problem with the transmissions used in our machines. Standing behind our machines and lacking sales, we were burning through cash. We slowed factory production with two furloughs and two layoffs, reducing our workforce by 30 percent.

Lessons learned

These events taught us several lessons. First, it was surprising how quickly the recession hit and how sharply sales and revenue declined almost overnight. Even in late 2008, signs indicated we would have a year of modest growth. By the following spring, we were forced to resize our production plan very quickly and reduce it by 40 percent.

Lesson number two: Listen to your dad and mentor. Dad always impressed upon us how important it is to have cash reserves for a "rainy day," and that lesson allowed us to survive 2009. We used our reserves to finance the losses instead of being forced to borrow money from a bank. A few businesses in our industry that operated too close to the line financially at the time did not fare as well and were forced to sell. Thanks to Dad's advice and the cash reserves we had, we were able to keep our family ownership and our independence.

Lesson number three: Think outside the box.

Despite having two layoffs, one each in the spring and fall of 2009, there still was not enough work to keep our employees busy. We were staring at the real possibility of laying off some of our best and longest-tenured employees. Dean and I were desperate. We began praying separately for wisdom, and both of us received the same answer from the Lord. We would send several work teams into our community to perform service work while they were on the company payroll. It worked, layoffs were avoided, and jobs were saved. The move served as a bridge into January, and soon thereafter, mower demand picked up. In 2010, we were also able to rehire many of the workers who had been laid off in 2009.

Lesson number four: You do not know the strength of your relationships until tested in a hard time. For 35 years, we maintained what we assumed was a solid relationship with our bank, one that had survived five bank mergers and acquisitions. That relationship was tested in 2009. Renewal of our seasonal line of credit was due just as we began to experience negative cash flow. Instead of offering much needed financial support, the bank pushed us to draconian terms and conditions for renewal. On the advice of our attorney, we looked for and found a new banking relationship. The new bank offered us a better program, which along with the cash reserves we had, helped us survive the recession and climb out of the 2009 financial hole.

There is a benefit that comes from having a problem. Relationships, partnerships, and cooperating with other businesses are not appreciated and strengthened until they are tested. Anyone can be your partner and friend when times are good and there are no problems. But you know a true partner is one who stays with you during a tough time.

Dignity of reply

Our company has always treasured long-term business relationships. One important part of building a relationship is having what I term "dignity of reply," family-style. We have always felt all inquiries, whether via a letter, email, phone call, or received in person deserve the dignity and respect of a reply. We do not screen calls, nor do we ever ignore requests for information.

Yes, some inquiries are less interesting than

others, and junk phone calls and junk mail are part of the mix if screening is not used. But when you screen or otherwise ignore inquiries, you may miss the one inquiry that could be the beginning of a needed business relationship. As a side note, we have a real live person answer the phone at our office. We believe a menu-driven response is disrespectful to humans.

Along with answering inquiries with respect, I learned early on the importance of being respectful and nonjudgmental to all people who would cross our path. When we were in the Power Truck business, an older Mennonite man stopped by the shop one day. He was neat and clean in appearance, but his bib overalls were patched, and he looked as if he would not have two nickels to rub together.

My dad began to show him the Power Truck and explain its design features. I noticed how my dad treated him with respect, the same respect he would show anyone else making an inquiry. Then my dad offered to let him take a test drive, which he did. The man took a short drive up and back down the country road by our factory and then pulled up in front of Dad.

"I think I take it," he said with a distinctive

German dialect, and we had another customer. I learned that day not to judge people by their appearance.

Day of rest

As a farmer/rancher, my grandpa Walker raised Registered Polled Hereford cattle. A sign at the entry of the farm read: Walker's Polled Herefords, Remember the Sabbath Day To Keep It Holy, No Sunday Sales. My grandpa took Sunday as his Sabbath day. He would take care of the animals on Sunday, but all other farming activity was done in six days.

Following Grandpa's example, four generations of our family have followed Sabbath observance as a principle. According to Scripture, we believe our Creator worked six days and rested from his work on the seventh. To honor our Creator, we rest from our work each seventh day.

Grandpa told us about the time he tried to harvest wheat on Sunday. The wheat had ripened and needed to be cut. One after another a series of breakdowns on his harvesting equipment left the wheat standing. Grandpa said he took that as a personal lesson; he never tried to cut wheat again on Sunday.

In the manufacturing business, we have tried to do our best to rest from our work on Sunday, without being legalistic in observance. The factory does not operate on Sunday, even when times demand it, and we avoid promoting our product at trade shows on Sunday. We get permission from show management to not man our display, and even though we miss a day of the show, we believe it is made up by contacts made during the other days. For our family, observing Sabbath is a principle, but we do not judge others who have a different way of living, either to observe Sabbath or not.

We also believe Sabbath rest is good for our employees' health and well-being and for the strengthening of their families. We believe it is in our DNA to require one day out of seven to rest, and believe those who ignore the principle and work seven days often end up paying the high price of losing instead of gaining.

CHAPTER 7

Independent Thinking

Growth should not take priority, rather it should
be the outcome of doing everything else right.

Some companies are so focused on growth that it becomes an obsession with them. Publicly traded companies especially, and their shareholders, are driven by the quarterly growth of their stock prices. The shareholder is a hard taskmaster who is only interested in one thing: multiplying money.

In contrast, privately-owned companies have the advantage of taking the long view and making decisions that are beneficial in the long term, including adjusting to changing economic seasons and marketplace opportunities. In times of challenge, my dad always liked to say, "The first objective is to stay in business; the second objective is to grow." Or to say it another way, some companies get so busy growing that they forget to stay in business. In our view, growth should not take priority, rather it should be the outcome of doing everything else right. Not obsessing about growth can be a great help and offer many benefits to the private business owner.

Growing too fast

One hazard of growing too fast is the potential to lose control of the company. In many ways, how much a company grows is directly proportional to how much money it wants to spend. Company owners can choose to finance growth with internal cash flow and grow more slowly, or they can accelerate it by bringing in cash from outside investors or bankers.

Once the investor holds more than 50 percent of the company, it is all over for private owners. They no longer have control, even if they have been told they do by the investor. As an entrepreneur, when you have lost financial control of your business, you have lost everything. At that point, you might as well go to work somewhere else for wages. This was my dad's experience in Casper, Wyoming, when he sold control of the Power Truck.

Growing too fast can also put a strain on the entire manufacturing process. I like to think of our manufacturing system and our product as the heart of our circulatory system, with our distributors, dealers, and customers making up its veins and arteries. If our distributors, dealers, and customers are flourishing, healthy, and have vitality, the "heart" (our manufacturing system) will be strong and healthy. Running too fast is to tax the system, and it will ultimately do more harm than good. Our mantra is: Grow slow, grow strong, and stay independent.

Having good instincts

When Dad sold the company and Power Truck in 1968, he imagined he would enjoy working in the company and letting the "professionals" take care of the operating headaches. Observing the new leaders, he began to realize his business instincts were better than he had once thought. When combined with the experience gained from previously running his own company, he had the strong desire to be independent again. After all, the desire to be independent was one of the reasons Dad left the family farming operation and started a manufacturing company in the first place.

Later, throughout the 11 years we worked with Byco manufacturing coolers, we still were not independent. We had only one customer, Byco, and were totally dependent on their health and well-being. If Byco went downhill, we were pretty sure they would take us down with them.

We watched with concern when on two or three occasions Byco brought in new business partners. These new partners assured us they were "silent partners," and everything would stay the same with the current management team. Unfortunately for Byco and us, the partners did not remain silent very long, and the results were not good.

In 1984, by going full-time with the Walker Mower, we became independent again and gained our freedom. Oh, happy day! Since then, almost every manufacturer in our industry has approached us with a buyout or merger offer, and in every case our answer has been "no." We remember our earlier experiences and are resolved to stay independent.

Carrot and a stick

The typical merger or acquisition offer comes with a carrot and a stick. The carrot? Join us and you will have more resources and more growth opportunities. The stick? If you choose otherwise, you may be squashed out of business by the "big boys." Despite offers, we have kept on track, working within our smaller "niche" market and staying fiercely independent. My dad liked to say, "I'd rather have my own hamburger stand than be a part of McDonald's."

Family-owned companies can jeopardize their independence in other ways. One of the more subtle ones is to lose control of the complete business cycle, production and marketing. For example, companies that retain another company to make their products and put their name on it (private label) are not independent because they cannot control the quality and cost of producing the product.

Loss of independence can also result from doing business with big retail companies like Home Depot or Walmart or employing other marketing channels separate from their own. It is a common story for a small, family-owned company to gear up to fulfill a contract with a big retailer only to discover the big retailer's market control dictates the price, terms, and conditions—often taking the small company to the point of bankruptcy.

Entrepreneurial vision

A smaller, independent company like Walker Manufacturing has one other distinct advantage over being associated with a big organization. There is the vision of an entrepreneur that is key to success, a vision that is often missing or stifled in large organizations. We can bring that vision to life. As an independent manufacturer, we like to do as much for ourselves as possible by insourcing instead of outsourcing. We do our own product design and development, and our own manufacturing. We put our name on the product, maintain financial control, and operate the business family-style.

Best of all, by being independent and in control, we can make our own decisions, fulfill our commitments, keep our promises, and protect and honor the investments of our distributors, dealers, and end-customers. We live and breathe the benefits of being an independent company.

CHAPTER 8

Your Best Opportunity

*There is nothing better than to be doing
what you were born to do.*

We believe it is important for each person to work to find his or her best opportunity. It is not unusual for people to struggle and experience false starts and dead ends before finding their best opportunity. I watched my dad work hard all his life on several different projects. Often, he had little to show for his effort except a lot of hard work. Finally, in developing and manufacturing the Walker Mower, all the hard work began to pay off. There is nothing better than to be doing what you were born to do, reach a point where you are working at your best opportunity, and to be rewarded for your effort.

How do you find your best opportunity? Some say it is out of our control and instead talk about luck and being in the right place at the right time. I prefer to think "good providence" from the Giver of all good things has a lot to do with it. Still, we all play a part in seeking because opportunities do not come to people who do nothing.

Certainly, persistence plays a role versus just settling for a job. Burgeoning entrepreneurs may never find their best opportunity if they are continually paralyzed by looking for the next "big" opportunity, forgetting to take advantage of what is right in front of them and forgetting to get started.

I believe the path to the best opportunity is often disguised by an unimpressive start and using the small resources at hand. I love the story about the Wright brothers who, in spending only about $1,000 in trial-and-error experiments, successfully invented the airplane. Compare that to aviation pioneer Samuel Langley and his team of professional engineers who spent $50,000 of the War Department's money to make an airplane that promptly fell into the Potomac

River on its initial attempt (no trial and error) to fly.

Our product

Why doesn't Walker Manufacturing design a mower that costs less and competes with some of the lower-priced mowers on the market? That is a fair question. The quick answer is we try to design equipment we would like to buy ourselves, and we just happen to have a taste for high-quality, high-performing equipment.

Our family members grew up willing to pay more to get more value because we think that equipment longevity and performance are important. Dean, the principal designer for the Walker Mower, understands how important this value is to our customers. One can see that in the mower's design and operation. As I mentioned in an earlier chapter, he is obsessed with the machine's performance, making it do the best at what it was designed to do, and he continuously works to improve on it. Dean also has a design focus on serviceability as evidenced by our mowers that have tilt-open bodies giving access to the drivetrain, tilt-up decks for servicing blades, and liberal use of grease fittings to lubricate moving parts. Dean is the epitome of persistence. He is never satisfied, never done with making improvements. In his mind, working and improving an earlier design takes priority over starting a new project.

In addition to building quality equipment, we think our best opportunity is to build machines that are not readily available on the market. For that reason, we have not jumped into building the popular designs of mid-mount riding mowers or stand-on mowers. The last thing the market needs is a copy of the mid-mount style machine or stand-on mower colored yellow and called a Walker. Instead, we have focused on our niche with the front-mount style machine and enjoy being known in the market as a "front-mount riding mower specialist."

Being a specialist

Being a specialist comes with the risk associated with shutting out a portion of the marketplace and not having the stability that manufacturers who cover a broader market have. Conversely, we would argue there is more strength and stability in doing a few things well than doing many things in a mediocre way.

For example, the Walker Mower is sent to markets around the world. We learn from our experiences there—with different grass types, climates, and cultural practices—how to improve on our one-mower design. We make a better machine today for all markets, including the USA, from this experience.

In some instances, we make a special mower deck design for a specific overseas market to improve performance in conditions quite different from what one finds in this country. It would be difficult, if not nearly impossible, to make these improvements if we manufactured a covey of different machines to satisfy every market.

Our philosophy has been to build durable, serviceable products that need local servicing dealers to give customers full value for their investment. For that reason, all our mowers are sold through a network of servicing dealers. We have no desire to build throwaway, disposable equipment (typically sold by mass merchants) even though that equipment category remains popular with many customers.

Becoming a servant-leader

We have become a strong competitor and leader in the commercial mowing business because we are both energetic and excited about producing a product that serves our customers. But I believe that's only part of what lies behind our success. There is an old saying: Leadership is earned and not given. And how is leadership earned? There is another old teaching (biblical) that is paraphrased: Whoever would become a leader, let him be a servant (Matthew 20:26). That sounds like a paradox, an approach that just would not work in the dog-eat-dog business world. Yet, this is a principle on which Walker Manufacturing was founded and has tried to follow.

Let me explain. In free enterprise, no one is forced to do business with our company. Our suppliers do not have to sell us components, and factory employees do not have to work here. Our distributors and dealers do not have to sell our products, and our customers do not have to buy them, either. It is all voluntary. A leader cannot lead if no one is willing to follow.

How successful a company becomes (and the leadership position it attains) hinges on the people who choose to entrust themselves to, and associate with, the company and its products. Because it is voluntary, the choice is largely based on how well the company serves the interests of others. By serving others, we indirectly help ourselves. And due to the trust placed in our company, leadership is attained. It is amazing how strong business relationships become when they are not forced, and when the basis of conduct is looking after the other party's interest as well as your own.

CHAPTER 9

Building a Foundation

*People often tell us that Walker Mower owners are
"like a family." After all, doesn't doing business
come down to this? People make businesses,
and people like to do business with people.*

At Walker Manufacturing, I like to think we
are building more than a mower. We are
building a business based on a rock-solid
foundation of principles. Being a servant-leader is
just one of them. There are others.

Being a good customer

Commercial mower manufacturers and their end-customers are at completely different ends of the production cycle. The manufacturer produces the product and the customer uses it. Simple as that, right? Because of this relationship, it is easy to think the two have little in common. To the contrary, they have a lot in common as many aspects of business development, operation, and management are the same.

The similarity is particularly striking when it comes to the kind of customers Walker Manufacturing and its mowing contractor customers want. After all, customers are the foundation of the business and are highly sought after as the most necessary ingredient to starting and sustaining the business.

So, what kind of customers do we both want? We both want:

1. Customers who are discriminating and who will pay a fair price for value received; not ones always looking for the cheapest price.

2. Customers who are loyal because of

continuing satisfaction with the product and service.

3. Customers, who by enthusiastic satisfaction, help win new customers by word-of-mouth advertising.

4. Customers who do their part to receive satisfaction (follow instructions, accept responsibility when responsible, and do not expect "freebies" for every little thing).

These customers exist! Walker Manufacturing has been fortunate to have more than our share. It brings to mind an old axiom that is one of the principles of our company foundation: To have good customers, you need to be a good customer.

Herein lies a contradiction we see among some landscape contractors. They want to be paid top dollar for their work and pay bottom dollar for their equipment purchase and equipment dealer service. If you are a landscape contractor and wondering where all the good customers are, the axiom might just point the way the next time you go shopping for equipment or work with your local dealer.

We have worked to be a good customer to our suppliers and to develop long-term relationships with them. While we do not want to pay more than we should, we do not constantly put our business relationships "out for bid" or pit one supplier's price against the other. When we have made an error, we do our best to take responsibility and our long-term suppliers reciprocate. We do our best to keep our commitments to our suppliers and pay our bills when due, not using the other guy's money for our cash flow.

It has been surprising to see the favorable treatment given to us from some of our biggest suppliers— they treat us like one of their big customers even when we know we are not. We especially treasure our relationships with two suppliers that go back 60 years, starting with the Walker Executive Golf Car: Kohler Engine Company, Kohler, Wisconsin, supplies our engines; and Farrar Corporation, Norwich, Kansas, supplies iron castings, machined parts, and axle assemblies.

Doing business family-style

At Walker Manufacturing, we view being family-owned and operated as a distinct advantage in the marketplace. Some large competitors might think otherwise, suggesting that smaller, family-run companies like ours lack the strength and stability they have.

But do larger competitors have the strength and stability they purport to have? Decades of mergers, consolidations, and downsizing in big corporate business point to a different conclusion. Being big is not necessarily synonymous with strength and stability. This is particularly true when a big company has lost its "family focus" and begins to treat people like a commodity.

Here is Walker Manufacturing's definition of what it takes to conduct business family-style:

1. Family-style recognizes the importance of each person's contribution to the company that goes well beyond our immediate family. Having concern for employees and their families, giving credit to others, and sticking together in good and bad times is part of our definition.

2. Family-style means taking care of each other. At Walker Manufacturing, policies such as year-round employment and no shift work

strengthen our employees' families. The principle we follow is: "Strong companies are built by strong persons; strong persons come from strong families, and strong families come from God's hand." Anything we can do to strengthen our families ultimately strengthens our company. This is not to say we only have strong people working in the company. But we try to operate the company in a way to help strengthen families.

3. Family-style within our company also spills over to our relationships with distributors, dealers, and end-customers. We are particularly pleased that many customers are private owners and small businesses where the family focus is important to them.

People often tell us that Walker Mower owners are "like a family." That is precisely what we have worked for and hoped for over the last 40 years. After all, doesn't doing business come down to this? People make businesses, and people like to do business with people.

Fear and faith

Life is unpredictable, filled with twists and turns. Who could have foretold the 2020 virus pandemic that became a huge challenge for people and businesses around the world? Even predictions themselves can be harmful, whether they come true or not. Remember Y2K? Alarmists and doomsayers predicted catastrophic problems, often profiting handsomely from fear of the future.

Either way, real or predicted, disasters cause people to live in fear of the future and the unknown. For the Walker family, our view of the future is more balanced and is based on our faith. We look at Holy Scripture and believe the future will bring both good and bad things into our company. We are people of optimism and hope. Yet, catastrophe and hard times may come, and human frailty may affect our progress and prosperity. As the Bible says, "For he makes his sun to rise on the evil and the good, and sends rain on the just and on the unjust" (Matthew 5:45b, ESV).

By faith, we believe God is in control. We face the

future with confidence and without fear. A favorite bit of wisdom from Holy Scripture sums it up for me and the Walker family: "He [a righteous man] will have no fear of bad news; his heart is steadfast, trusting in the Lord" (Psalm 112:7 NIV, 1978).

Answering the big question

"Why am I in business?" is a big question that needs a good answer. Why do people start a business knowing there are risks? Not only are there risks, but there are challenges associated with birthing it and then operating it. Yet for entrepreneurs like my dad, being independent and bringing new ideas to life far outweighed the risks and challenges. Walker Manufacturing is the result of his dream and hard work.

Of course, there are other reasons to start a business, just as there are reasons to stay in business. Some would say they are in business to make a profit (multiply money). But to us, for all that it takes to be in business, that is not a very satisfying answer. Dad fulfilled his dream and created opportunities for himself and his family, and we want to continue to build on his legacy by creating more opportunities for our family and others. From that legacy the most satisfying answer to the question of why we are in business is found in looking at all the opportunities being created by one small company in Colorado, USA.

For us, it is exciting to be in the manufacturing business and to see the ripple effect of creating a livelihood and opportunities for many other people besides the immediate Walker family. Our suppliers, factory employees, distributors, dealers, and end-customers all have an opportunity that would not exist if Walker Manufacturing were not in business.

Why are we in business, then? Creating multiple opportunities is a satisfying answer for us and should be for anyone, including many of our end-customer business owners who want to create opportunities for their families and the families of their employees.

There is a principle of multiplication found in the Bible (John 6:5-14) that shows the way God works, and it is perfectly illustrated by Jesus feeding 5,000 people from one boy's small lunch of five loaves and two fish. The same principle is at work today when we see that God uses multiplication of resources that are given to Him to meet people's needs. At Walker, we believe when we give our little "lunch" to the Lord, thousands are fed by our business. This is when it gets exciting to be in business.

Years ago, I heard an expression that made a lot of sense, especially for company owners. "Love people, use money, instead of love money, use people." The first way speaks to the way I have been taught by my parents and the way my brother Dean and I have tried to operate Walker Manufacturing. To us, loving people means taking care of people. Using money means money that is accumulated in business becomes a tool to multiply opportunities mentioned above. We often think about the multiplication that has happened in our lives coming from our little lawn mower project 40 years ago.

Living the other way, where money is loved and people are used, is a disaster. Unfortunately, many modern business models seem to be based on using people (when you need them and sending them away when you don't) all in the name of efficiency, operating "lean," and maximizing profits. Most of us have experienced firsthand or observed the shipwreck that happens when a company or a family loses their way and loving money kicks in. It gets real ugly really fast, and every kind of evil emerges.

Over the years, our wish for all our customers has been for them to love people and use money, and see how multiplication works in their lives. Nothing thrills us more than to hear from our customers that the Walker Mower is helping them create multiplied opportunities for themselves and others.

Another observation about money—in our experience, we have found that when people let you know they have plenty of money by saying "money is no problem," it is a problem.

Humble beginnings

In the mid-1990s, Rod Dickens, the editor of *Walker Talk* magazine, and I were invited to attend a landscape contractor association meeting in Pennsylvania. We gave short presentations on the history of the Walker Mower and the evolution of the magazine. Afterward, an attendee raised his hand and asked Rod what it would take to be profiled in the magazine and if there are any pre-qualifications such as company size and type of customer. Rod answered,

"We do stories about all kinds of contractors, large and small alike. In fact, we recently did a story on a schoolteacher/contractor in Oklahoma."

The attendee, a Pennsylvania contractor, shot back, "We don't like schoolteachers; they are moonlighters." Knowing that many businesses are started on a part-time basis, I asked him how he got started. He would not answer my question. After the meeting, even the association president told us he had been a schoolteacher and had started his business working part-time.

I suspect that ego plays a role here. It seems that many business owners are reticent to admit their humble beginnings, and that includes starting out part-time on a shoestring and a prayer. Also, many do not want to mention this is the second time around or that there is a bankruptcy or loss of ownership in their business history. Yet, that is often the real story of business startups. We applaud the American dream, that we have the freedom to start our own business, that entrepreneurs-in-the-making are still being born every day, and that those who come here from other countries can work from humble beginnings and become successful, as well.

Not everyone who dreams of starting their own

business makes the decision to do so. One of the primary reasons they hesitate is the risk of failure. Unlike publicly-owned and government operations, private businesses face this real risk; there are no bailout plans or safety nets for them. (Of course, the owner should do everything possible to minimize risk.) The risk can result in bankruptcy or, as with us in the Power Truck business, selling of ownership.

On this point I like to quote business author Jim Collins from an article entitled, "The Secret of Enduring Greatness." He wrote, "Companies do not fall primarily because of what the world does to them or because of how the world changes around them; they fall first and foremost because of what they do to themselves." In other words, wrote Collins, success or failure "depends more on what you do to yourself than on what the world does to you."[1]

Risks become very real during hard times. Since starting the company, we have lived through several financial crises, including the Great Recession of 2008. Throughout, our response has mirrored Collins' advice of making sure we do not contribute to our own failure. During hard times our response has always been to:

1. Stay on course inside the company
2. Operate on the values and principles that have brought us this far
3. Endure the hard times by doing our best work

One of the principles Dad taught Dean and me was about being in business during hard times. The first objective, he said, was to "Stay in business."

CHAPTER 10

Beliefs Guide Us

What you believe in does make a difference,
and you can be sincerely wrong.

I n 2007, we developed the list "What We Believe at Walker." This was our attempt to communicate and remind us, our employees, and others outside the company about our core ideology, a clear definition of our operating principles, and what we stand for. It is important to note that while our beliefs were not written down in the beginning, we have lived the foundational beliefs and developed others from experience as we have operated the business across the years. These are lived-out beliefs.

In the modern world, it is not popular to believe anything with certainty, dependability, and absolute truth and moral foundation. Rather, beliefs are to be tinkered with, taken apart, examined, and repackaged to accommodate diversity, tolerance, and choice. The thinking is that all beliefs are of equal value, and it does not matter what you believe, as long as you sincerely believe in something.

We disagree with the thinking of the foregoing paragraph with old-fashioned certainty. What you believe does make a difference, and you can be sincerely wrong. We know. We have had a few wrong ideas ourselves. Beliefs are important to guide a happy, healthy, satisfying life, and in the same way, they guide a successful business.

The ancient biblical text (James 1:5-8) speaks of a "double-minded" person who doubts and does not believe, as one who is unstable, driven, and tossed by every wind and wave. That person is incapable of receiving wisdom from God, the text says. When a person or business does not have beliefs (the great overarching ideas) of who you are, why you are here, and what your operating principles are, that person or business misses the opportunity to be guided in daily activities and to have a meaningful life.

In this changing world, our beliefs are constantly being challenged. There is great value in testing the situations faced against beliefs. There is also great value in passing them along to the next generation who will guide the company into the future.

Our beliefs:

- Operate by principles that are optimum for employees and their families.
- Promises are to be kept; keep your word, tell the truth, be honest in all things (Dishonesty cannot be tolerated within the company or in outside relationships, as it is ultimately destructive).
- Pursue excellence in all work without excuse. The results of this pursuit are easily seen in every part of the business and in all relationships both inside and outside the company.
- Opportunity to lead depends on serving our suppliers, employees, and customers, all who voluntarily associate themselves with the company based on how well we serve them.
- Remember where our help and blessings come from. Live and work with gratitude for all the

Lord has done for us.

- Trial and error is powerful in finding the right way. Keep your experiments on a small scale, so in error, the damage is small scale.

- Understand that the primary objective of the business is to produce multiplied opportunities; multiplying money is further down the list and is more of a means to the primary objective.

- Never allow growth to be the main goal. It is an outcome from doing everything else right.

- In all relationships, show mercy and forgiveness since the Lord has been merciful and forgiving to us.

- The Lord's Sabbath day will be honored by resting from our work.

- Your most equitable path is to honor, consider, and protect the investments of others as if they were your own (consider employees, suppliers, marketers, and customers).

- Always love people, use money.

- By working together as a company of people, we can accomplish a better livelihood for ourselves than available by working individually; helping others succeed builds your own success.

- Our Lord God, our Senior Partner, has given us this opportunity. We are stewards of the business, the opportunity, and the culture. We will operate by principles and ways to honor His name.

- Unrelenting loyalty to customers builds long-term relationships. A strong product opens the door while good service keeps it open.

- Never ignore a request. All requests or inquiries deserve the dignity of a reply. Do not screen or selectively not respond. In doing so you may miss the one opportunity you truly needed.

- Dignity and honor exist in all work performed by diligent workers—as much as each person should be working at their best opportunity, take pride in their work, and enjoy what they are doing.

- Stay independent. Use internally generated finance, product development, and in-house production to keep control and build continuing opportunity.

Staying enthused

I think it was 10 years ago when my lovely wife Barbara and I celebrated our 44th wedding anniversary in Hawaii. The time comes to mind as I recall how a waitress named Maggie Rose impressed us with her enthusiastic attitude.

As the menus were handed out, she let us know the ribs were "the best you'll ever eat." Later, I overheard her tell another couple who asked what was good on the menu, "It's all good." Then, when our order was taking a longer time than normal to come out from the kitchen, she brought us a couple of small bowls of chips for our eight grandkids, to tide them over until the food arrived. She told them, "Don't eat too much because you are going to want to eat all of the wonderful brisket sandwiches that you ordered." She was right. It was a good meal, but her enthusiasm was what made it a wonderful experience and made us glad we chose to eat there.

As we were leaving, I asked Maggie Rose how long she had worked there. She told me she had been there one-and-a half years and had worked 15 years as a waitress overall, long enough for me to know her enthusiasm was not a beginner's glow and was time-tested.

This kind of enthusiasm is not so much a feeling as it is an attitude. There will be hard days and problems in any restaurant, but enthusiasm will stay with people who believe in what they are doing and who they are working with. I got the idea that Maggie Rose is a person who would not work at a restaurant if she could not brag about the food being served.

My pastor had a saying that rang true along this line. "If you want to stay married a long time, stay enthused about your spouse." All of us who have been married a long time know that this enthusiasm is more than just a feeling. It is an attitude that stays with the ups and downs of living, knowing that regardless of the circumstances, you married the right person. This is your best opportunity, your best path.

Staying enthused is a great way to live, both in your personal life and in your vocation or business life. Enthusiasm is the oil that keeps all the machinery of life moving along. After more than four decades of building Walker Mowers, I am still enthused about being in the manufacturing business and being in an independent, family-owned business. I am still enthused about the Walker Mower, a product that helps our customers make beautiful places. And I am enthused about the multiplied opportunities that have come from supplying more than 170,000 Walker Mowers to customers around the world.

Creating jobs

Before the pandemic of 2020 hit and put millions of workers out of a job, unemployment in the country had seen both highs and lows, and the topic of how to create jobs continues to be a timely one for politicians. There are two ways to create jobs: through the public sector (government) and the private sector (private business).

Some government leaders seem to think the best way to create jobs is through the public sector. But do government-created jobs offer the same economic opportunity as private enterprise? I think not. First, public-sector jobs are funded by taxpayers where money is taken from one pocket (borrowed) and given to another pocket. No real multiplication or incentives are found here.

By contrast, private-sector jobs are created by offering goods and services on the free market where consumers can pick the best value and will pay a profit (not a dirty word) to the business. Profit attracts capital (capitalism) to be invested because of the incentive for growth and return on investment. In addition, competition in the free market raises the proposition that offering the best products and services and working harder will present even more opportunities in private business.

The bottom line is, with a relatively small investment to start a private business, and with lots of hard work and with God's help, multiplication takes place and thousands of jobs are created. Incidentally, I believe God ordained business in the beginning when He told the first people to subdue the earth, to multiply, and to be the master over creation (Genesis 1:28).

Talking about multiplication in private business brings up a second point. Private business creates wealth while government enterprises do not. Wealth creation is good and fuels the economic engine of private enterprise. It should be remembered that wealth creation comes from business, and that wealthy people create jobs; poor people do not. I am more than a little tired of being told by some government leaders that wealthy people are not "paying their fair share" and "need to pay more." I believe these leaders are out of touch and fail to understand the connection between wealth creation and job creation in private business.

Small, slow beginnings

When we started building our first lawn mower prototype, we had challenged ourselves to see if we could make a better lawn mower than was currently on the market. That is all we were doing. We called it a "hobby project" since our main livelihood at the time was manufacturing tractor cab coolers for another company. As I said earlier, we had no grand plan to get into the lawn mower manufacturing business.

Several years later, when the tractor cab cooler business came to a sudden end, we had to go full-time in the lawn mower business to survive. Once making the commitment, it took several more years before the business became profitable and we began to grow. Now, 40 years later, this business has become the best opportunity we have ever had since my parents started manufacturing in the 1950s.

At the time we started the lawn mower project, we had no idea it would become our best opportunity. I think an important lesson can be learned from this. Quite often, opportunities are missed because of the human tendency to look for big opportunities, and to be impatient and dismissive with what appears to be small. An ancient prophecy from biblical text gives the counterintuitive wisdom for those seeking opportunity. "Who dares despise the day of small things?" (Zechariah 4:10 NIV, 1978). In context, this question may be restated and paraphrased as: Do not despise small beginnings. Bigger opportunities often come for those who will start with what (little) they have and move ahead to claim what they could not see in the beginning.

Successful business owners often share a common bond: a small, slow start. Some people start a mowing business just to "fill in" until they can find a "real job." Then they discover they really enjoy the business of making beautiful places, working outdoors, and being their own boss. Ultimately, the story ends with these risk-takers realizing a much bigger opportunity than they ever imagined.

The other people who are exciting to watch are young people (next generation) who often have no choice but to start small and slow. It is exciting to watch these dreamers who virtually build an opportunity out of nothing. We can identify with both groups and anyone else who starts small and slow, because that describes our beginnings, as well.

CHAPTER 11

Working Together

Relationships do count and it is worthwhile work to build them.

I t has always been our idea (going all the way back to when Dad led the company) that everyone in the company is working primarily for themselves and their families. What better way to make a better livelihood than to join forces and work together with other workers toward a common goal?

With that in mind, we like to say to our employees that they work "with" us instead of "for" us. We believe this understanding of working together benefits the employees and their families in several ways and that helping others succeed builds your own success.

This is more than rhetoric. We want employees to have a job they can depend on to support their families. To provide full-time, year-round jobs, we have chosen to operate with level manufacturing, producing machines at a steady rate all year long even though the product demand is seasonal.

Seasonal or temporary jobs do not exist in our company, which is one reason why many of our workers come here and stay a long time. The average tenure working with Walker Manufacturing is 11 years. This not only pays off for the employees; it pays off for the company, too, by having workers who are invested in their jobs and understand that doing their best work today helps them have a continuing opportunity in the future.

Employees put in a standard nine-hour workday and have a strong work ethic. The standard 45-hour week gives them five hours of overtime pay. In addition to raising employees' compensation, the extra hours benefit the company by reducing headcount. Also, since we are a production company, all factory workers receive 1.5 hours of "on-time-full-time" bonus pay each week for being on-time and working the full schedule.

Several employees have logged consecutive perfect-attendance years, and one of our welders has celebrated 15 consecutive years. In contrast to those who complain about the work ethic of millennials, nearly half of our factory team is comprised of millennials. They show up every day and work just as hard as our more senior workers. Over the years, we have also avoided shift work so employees can spend quality time with their families.

Until the 2020 pandemic, unemployment in northern Colorado was at historic lows. Despite the high labor demand from energy producers and builders in our area, we have been able to fill all open positions without using recruiters or agencies. A high percentage of our job applicants are referrals from family and friends of employees.

The next time you see a Walker Mower, please think of a group of hands-on workers in Colorado who love making things while providing for their families. Work is work, but when you work "with" instead of "for" a company, there is more enjoyment and pride, knowing end-customers are receiving your best effort. Our workers want customers to receive top quality and value for their investment. That is a good feeling for them to have and something for which we are very proud.

Having a good name

Ancient wisdom teaches that a good name is one of the most valuable assets of a business (and for each of us personally). The Holy Bible states that "A good name is more desirable than great riches; to be esteemed is better than silver or gold" (Proverbs 22:1 NIV, 1978). Another bit of common wisdom is that it takes a long time to build a good name and it only takes a few minutes to destroy one. Consider some of the once-great company names in our country that now are jeered and berated because they were caught in fraud. Their formerly good name is now trash and has no value in the marketplace. Certainly, we have all seen examples of this on the personal level, as well.

Great company names and brands can lose their luster in ways other than committing fraud. Being sold is one of these ways. When we entered the lawn mower industry, one of the well-known brand names was Dixon. The original family owners eventually sold their company to a bigger corporation, only to be sold again and finally purchased by another big company in the industry. After a few more years, that company discontinued the Dixon brand and its product line. That was the end of the line, literally, for Dixon. The once-valuable name went to zero value.

How is a good name built? I would suggest three behaviors that work to make a name and reputation extremely valuable:

1. **Rugged honesty.** Truth telling, promise keeping, and rock-solid dependability have always been the foundation for building a good name.
2. **Serving well.** The only reason that any of us have an opportunity in business and ask to be paid for our work is based on how well we serve. In this sense, all businesses are in the "service industry."
3. **Staying with it.** Great names are not built overnight, but with consistency over time. Money can neither buy a good name nor buy out the time factor required for building a good name.

Showing gratitude/being generous

Living with gratitude is based on our attitude and outlook. It is a choice we make to recognize the good provisions and opportunities that have come to us. It is understanding where our help comes from, and being thankful to those who have helped us and to our God who created us. When we are grateful, we want to be generous, passing along the blessings to others and giving away the surplus. I like to think that gratitude and generosity are two sides of the same coin.

The old adage, "Actions speak louder than words" applies here. Dean and I and our sisters would say that our parents did not talk so much about being generous, but they did model it for us; we saw their actions. In this way, generosity is not advertised, but is quiet and part of the family's DNA to be passed from generation to generation.

When I think of generosity, I often remember one of my heroes, Mr. R.G. LeTourneau, reaching the point of giving 90 percent of his income to the Lord. I liked his saying, "I shovel (money) out, and

God shovels it back—but God has a bigger shovel." You can't out-give the Lord.

Being dependable

Two sayings, "You can count on me" and "One thing you can always count on is change," are not only mutually incompatible, but hardly generate reassurance for your customers and other stakeholders. We have all seen businesses and opportunities swept away even as they were telling their stakeholders they were dependable.

One of the keys to staying in business a long time is to be dependable, staying the same in all the important ways while keeping up with the changing world. We continue to work to reassure our stakeholders about their future with Walker, knowing they will see changes and a different look from time-to-time but knowing the "person" of the company (values, ethics, family ownership) will stay the same. Keeping control of the company and maintaining family ownership are among our best efforts to ensure our dependability well into the future.

Building strong relationships

The underpinnings of a strong business relationship are based on two great biblical principles: 1) Treat others as you wish to be treated (Luke 6:31), and 2) Look not only to your own interests but to the interests of others (Philippians 2:4, see the NIV 1978 translation of this verse). Great guidance comes from making business decisions when these two principles are considered, and there is tremendous strength in business relationships when these principles are lived out.

Integrity is the foundation for developing a long-term, loyal relationship. The great free enterprise principle is this: If integrity is compromised, your opportunity to be in business will end sooner or later. The essentials of integrity in business are truth telling, keeping your word and your commitments, and using fair exchange (fair prices and fair profits). Finally, it can be asked, "What are you accomplishing if customers are going out the back door as fast as they are coming in the front door because of your lack of integrity?"

It takes more than a few people to manufacture lawn mowers and have distributors and dealers to provide sales and service to customers all over the world. Relationships do count and it is worthwhile work to build them. The strength of a team is based on the strength of its relationships. What was accomplished in the past has depended on relationships, and what will be accomplished in the future will depend on relationships.

Continuing investment

When growing up, I thought about perpetual motion and wondered why it was not possible to make a machine that would keep running by itself without additional power input. At the time, I was unaware that the law of nature about "drag" and "friction" is what stops this dream from happening.

Another law, one taught in the Bible, applies similarly to business. Whoever sows sparingly will also reap sparingly, and whoever sows generously will also reap generously (2 Corinthians 9:6). Both laws counter the idea of investing little or nothing into something and yet hoping to strike it rich or reap a windfall. In the world of outdoor power equipment, some manufacturers, distributors, and dealers have fallen into thinking they could put little or no investment into their product or service and somehow, magically, they would harvest a big windfall of profits for their business.

Just like it takes the input of additional energy to keep a machine going, it takes additional investments to keep a business going. In his book *Good to Great*, Jim Collins talks about the flywheel principle in business, where the continuing push on the flywheel (investment) slowly builds momentum for the business. It is not one big explosive moment that turns the flywheel. The same holds true in business. Persistent work and investment in a business builds momentum, without which a nice payback on the investment and the breakthrough that moves a business from "good to great," would not be possible.

From our perspective, Walker Manufacturing is committed to continually invest in our best opportunity with the Walker Mower. We believe our best days are ahead, and we will see a time of "reaping" a bigger harvest. To name a few areas of continuing investment, we will be advancing our product design, improving efficiency of manufacturing, providing product sales training for distributors and dealers, and developing powerful marketing and merchandising tools and materials for our dealers.

Manufacturing technology

It is amazing how much technology is now available for manufacturing compared to the simple tools my dad started with. But just because the technology is available does not mean it always makes sense to use it. The volume of production needs to be balanced with the technology. In other words, technology needs to pay for itself. Low volume requires using less technology and high volume, more technology.

Certainly, to be competitive, the appropriate level of technology must be applied; our competitors will use technology to their benefit even if we choose not to. We like to say that we want our workers to be competitive with other workers around the world by putting the best possible tools and technology in their hands.

We have made it very clear that our reason for being in business is to create opportunities for people. We love people. Sometimes, using technology replaces people and reduces opportunities available to them. Just as production needs to be in balance with technology, so do people. Our mantra is to use technology when appropriate and skilled craftsmen when appropriate.

With that said, technology is always improving and will continue to displace workers along the way. To take care of their people, manufacturers must offer and provide (re)training so employees can continue to have opportunities with them and be part of the labor market.

There is no question that changes brought about by advancing technology can be disruptive and uncomfortable, especially for the older generation. For those who do not want to change or adapt, opportunities will be lost. My suggestion to them is to develop an attitude shared by lifelong students who retain their curiosity and are always willing to learn. I have enjoyed and admired people in their 70s and 80s who are still taking courses of study.

Switching roles and best opportunities

I came to work with the company with a degree in mechanical engineering. Dean has a degree in business administration. In the beginning, I was doing some design engineering work on the Byco coolers, along with having several other assignments. It did not take long, however, for me to realize my brother was gifted as a machine designer, something he had inherited from our dad. I was a textbook engineer; Dean had the design engineering gift.

Dean took the lead in designing the first Walker Mower prototype with my dad working alongside of him. Fairly quickly, I could see that my role in the company needed to move away from engineering, allowing Dean to take the lead in product design and development. I began to shift my focus to business operations and finance. When we decided to develop our own marketing program for the lawn mower, I took the assignment even though I had no formal training in marketing.

So, Dean and I switched disciplines. We found our best opportunities and discovered gifts that have created both enjoyment and personal challenges while working together over the last 45 years.

Skateboards

Like my dad before, when he built the miniature bulldozer and showed his machine-building ability, my brother Dean began building powered sit-down skateboards when he was in junior high. This unique machine is a cross between a go-kart and skateboard with skate steering (turn by leaning) and powered by a one-horsepower engine. The rider sits a few inches above the pavement and gets a thrilling ride scooting along at four to five miles per hour.

In later years, Dean has continued to build the skateboards, and several times we have thought about bringing them to market. We even got a design patent and made a few sample units back in the '70s. The thing that stopped us is the recent trends of product liability and putting the company in jeopardy with accident claims. Lots of fun products have not made it to the market or have been taken off the market because of our litigious society and personal injury attorneys aplenty.

Skateboards have even been part of our Family Reunion celebrations. We built a batch of eight and have had some very enjoyable entertainment for our attendees as they navigate the hay-bale road course in our parking lot.

Beautiful places

We have a little saying that gives perspective on the Walker Mower. "We don't make lawn mowers; we make beautiful places." It is not the machine, but what the machine does that makes it an exciting product. Some would question how we can get so excited about what we make at Walker Manufacturing. After all, it's only a lawn mower. But creating beautiful places for people to enjoy lends to the mower's higher calling and what we do. After all, when God created the first humans, He took them to a beautiful place and told them to take care of it, the Garden of Eden.

The journey

It is exciting for Dean and me to see Ted and Ryan leading the company with new energy and new approaches that will lead to new opportunities (new blood). My two nephews have made the following covenant with Dean and me: "We will lead the business according to the principles and beliefs that Max and Margaret lived by and that Bob and Dean have perpetuated, and we will hand the company to a fourth generation as it was handed to us."

Writing *The Walker Way* has given me the opportunity to tell our story and share a collected set of experiences and principles. But the Walker Way is more than that—it is the path we have walked and the journey we have taken, and we expect to keep walking. There is an old saying, "Life is a journey and not a destination," (attributed to Ralph Waldo Emerson) that helps keep the perspective of keeping on. Certainly, building a manufacturing company from scratch like my parents did was a journey and not a destination—and the journey has not ended. What a privilege it has been to live the Walker Way experience and see that it continues.

Epilogue

As I've reflected on my family after writing this book, I realize how much Scripture has served as a foundation for our family and our business. My dad was an ardent and enthusiastic student of the Bible his whole life and had memorized many of the Scriptures. Dad's favorite translation of the Bible was the King James Version, with its Old English rendering.

He would quote Scripture as it applied to current circumstances and events, trying to encourage people in their faith and walk of life. It seems to me that he had a verse for every occasion, something that I want to encourage others to do as they put today's events in the context of what God's Word says.

Here are four of my dad's favorite Bible verses, all from the King James Version:

"I will lift mine eyes unto the hills, from whence cometh my help. My help cometh from the Lord, which made heaven and earth" (Psalm 121:1-2).

"For I am not ashamed of the gospel of Christ: For it is the power of God unto salvation to every one that believeth; to the Jew first, and also to the Greek" (Romans 1:16).

"The Lord hath done great things for us, whereof we are glad" (Psalm 126:3).

"Trust in the Lord with all thine heart; and lean not unto thine own understanding. In all thy ways acknowledge him, and he shall direct thy paths" (Proverbs 3:5-6).

My own favorite verses from the Bible include the following from the New International Version, 1978:

"But seek first his kingdom and his righteousness, and all these things will be given to you as well" (Matthew 6:33).

"Look not only to your own interests but to the interests of others" (Philippians 2:4).

"He (a righteous man) will have no fear of bad news; his heart is steadfast, trusting in the Lord" (Psalm 112:7).

"The righteous person may have many troubles, but the Lord delivers him from them all" (Psalm 34:19).

One of my goals for the readers of our story is to encourage them to find foundational Scriptures for their own lives. These could be passed down through the generations of your family and find their way into your family story—in the same way that they found their way into ours. If our story can encourage one person and one family to build their lives on the Scriptures, it will have been well worth writing this book.

Endnotes

[1] Collins, Jim. "The Secret of Enduring Greatness," *Fortune* magazine, May 5, 2008.

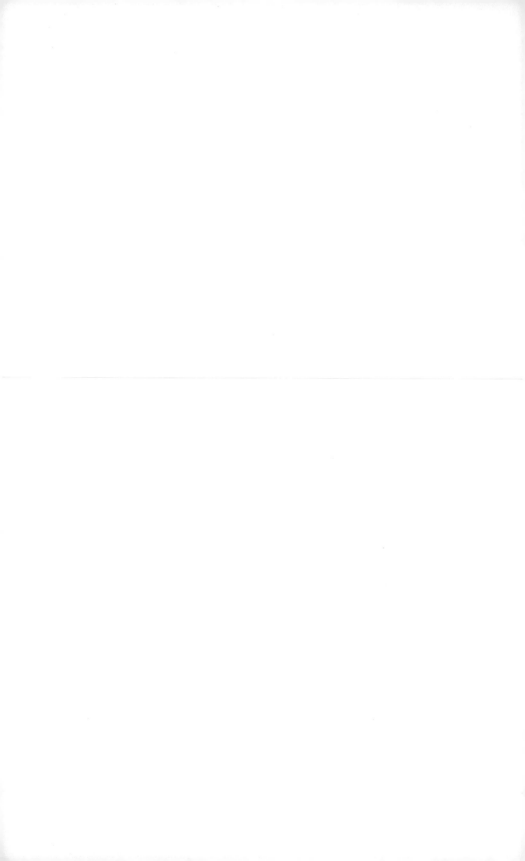

About the Author

 Bob Walker is the former president of Walker Manufacturing Company, and now as chairman, he continues to help lead all facets of business operations. He is a 1969 graduate of LeTourneau College with a degree in Mechanical Engineering. Bob worked for six years with Cessna Aircraft in Wichita, Kansas, before joining Walker Manufacturing Company in 1975.

Bob and Barbara, his wife of 54 years, have three lovely daughters and three wonderful sons-in-law. Nine beautiful grandchildren plus one grandson-in-law round out their family at this time. In his spare time, Bob enjoys flying small airplanes, singing in choirs and quartets, and traveling with his family. Bob and Barbara make their home in Fort Collins.

Additional Resources

For more information about the publisher, visit www.MultiplicationPublishing.com.

For bulk purchasing options, as well as bonus material and information about the book, visit www.TheWalkerWay.com. Make yourself at home, and be sure to sign our online guestbook.

To learn more about the Walker mower, visit www.Walker.com.